fishing for a Laugh

Fishing
for a Laugh

Reel
Humor
from
Alaska

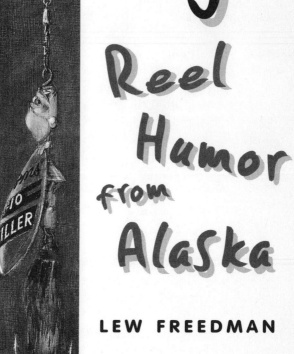

LEW FREEDMAN

EPICENTER PRESS
Seattle ▪ Fairbanks

Epicenter Press, Inc., is a regional press founded in Alaska whose interests include but are not limited to the arts, history, environment, and diverse cultures and lifestyles of the North Pacific and high latitudes. We seek both the traditional and innovative in publishing nonfiction tradebooks, contemporary art and photography giftbooks, and destination travel guides emphasizing Alaska, Washington, Oregon, and California.

Editor: Tricia Brown
Illustrator: Sandy Jamieson
Mapmaker: L.W. Nelson
Proofreader: Lois Kelly
Cover design: Elizabeth Watson
Inside design: Sue Mattson

Library of Congress Catalog Card Number: 97-078445
ISBN 0-945397-67-4

To order single copies of *Fishing for a Laugh*, mail $14.95 (Washington residents add $1.29 sales tax) plus $5.00 for first-class mailing to: Epicenter Press, Box 82368, Kenmore, WA 98028.

Booksellers: Retail discounts are available from our distributor: Graphic Arts Center Publishing, Box 10306, Portland, OR 97210. Phone 800-452-3032.

First printing April 1998
10 9 8 7 6 5 4 3 2 1
PRINTED IN CANADA

Contents

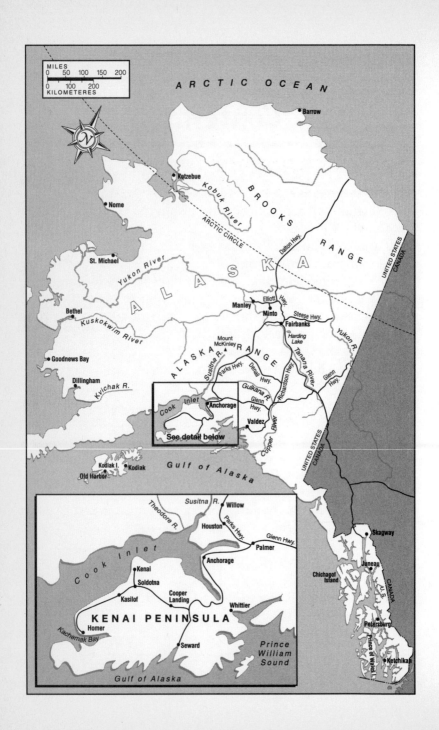

Acknowledgments

Thank you to all the fishermen and fishing guides who contributed stories of their experiences to this book. And a special thanks for extra, beyond-the-call help to Reuben Hanke and Charlotte Van Zyle.

Introduction
Is There Life Beyond Fishing?

You may have seen the T-shirt that reads *Fishing is Life*.

Nowhere is that message taken more seriously than Alaska.

The official state sport may be dog mushing, but that's only because fishing is not considered a sport. Fishing is way too important to the daily rhythms of Alaskan life to be lumped together with football, basketball and baseball, and the like.

So important that the phrase uttered by avid fisherwoman Charlotte Van Zyle deserves a T-shirt of its own: *I Fish, Therefore I Lie.*

There is at least some truth in that premise.

If you fish, then there is a very good chance that you exaggerate. Everyone is Pinocchio on the river. Must be something in the water. Or the air. The big one that got away? Gets bigger every day. The big one you caught? Gets bigger every day. The big one being mounted? Gets bigger every day. Why stop at fifty inches?

What we are saying here is that anyone who fishes, anyone who reads about fishing, or anyone who tells stories about fishing, enters the fray with a willing suspension of disbelief.

And it doesn't matter!

Kind of like politics, no one actually expects anyone who fishes to tell the gospel truth. You want the truth, go listen to sworn court testimony. You won't catch fishermen or fishing guides telling tales with right hand placed on the Bible. Perjury is not in the vocabulary of a man who totes around rod and reel.

That said, almost anyone who ever tells a fishing story claims it is the absolute, unvarnished truth. The only clue you might ever get that a particular story could be a stretch is if the teller announces beforehand, "True story." Otherwise you are on your own.

There is a rule that if you live in Alaska you must fish. You know how Alaskans are given something like a thousand dollars a year just for breathing? It's called the Permanent Fund Dividend check, and it's oil money. State officials take the check back if you don't fish. True story.

Nah, just kidding. I was testing you. There is no rule, just a bunch of pressure to fish. Fish or we'll force your kids to transfer schools.

I know this is true because once I prided myself on being The Only Person In Alaska Who Does Not Fish.

I didn't fish when I was a kid. My dad didn't fish. Close relatives didn't fish. So what did I know from fishing? Growing up, I didn't even eat fish. Give me burgers and fries every time. It was quite a responsibility being the only guy in Alaska who didn't fish. I was not anti-fishing. At the time I viewed myself more as a conscientious objector in the fish wars. I was Switzerland, taking no sides.

But the pressure built, I found myself getting intrigued, and beyond all that I came to love eating salmon steaks and deep-fried halibut. Pretty soon friends start to consider you a leech and hide the goodies in a padlocked freezer when they see you coming. When they take out billboards on Northern Lights Boulevard in Anchorage shouting "Get Your Own Fish!" you get the message.

Having no fishing background except the occasional TV remote scan alighting on Jimmy Houston's show, I thought I would start small. Jumping in and going after halibut, which can grow to the size of a Ford Explorer, and king salmon, which are often larger than fourth-graders, seemed a mite intimidating. So I went to pet stores to check out the goldfish. They seemed more my speed.

There were no fishing charters leaving anytime soon. In fact, you could pretty much scoop up all the goldfish you wanted with a big spoon. Not much challenge, I admit. Some people took home gobs of goldfish as pets. But some people took home gobs of goldfish for dinner. Not for themselves, but to feed their piranha. Not my thing.

You can walk into a department store, office building, barber shop, pretty much anywhere in Alaska and stumble upon a wall decoration consisting of a mounted, trophy king salmon. Some people like oil paintings, some people like sports posters, some people like fish staring at them with beady little eyes. This is a common sight in Alaska.

Less common is a mounted goldfish, though I was assured by the operator of aptly named Hunter Fisher Taxidermy that people do mount dearly departed goldfish. (I thought they flushed them down the toilet.) The man had only recently mounted a three-inch goldfish named Arnold on a walnut plaque. I believe he said "True story" when he told me about it. Arnold had no comment.

Anyway, after doing all this research I realized goldfish fishing would not bring me the necessary prestige to be enshrined in the angler's hall of fame. Lots of people in Alaska fish for rainbow trout, grayling, Arctic char, and the like. But if you do not fish for king salmon, silver salmon, red salmon, and halibut, you might as well go to a restaurant to place your dinner order. Those are the fish that really count in Alaska.

You must realize that up until I was in my thirties I thought all salmon came in a can. Woody Allen once wrote an essay in which he said he went tuna fishing with Ernest Hemingway and caught four cans. I identified. (Of course, I knew he was lying because I had been to a supermarket without Ernest Hemingway and taken home ten cans on sale.)

At long last I broke down and made plans to go fishing. Alaska has the best fishing in the world. There is lake fishing, river fishing, and ocean fishing. The Kenai River is home to the world's largest king salmon, and it is located about 150 miles south of Anchorage by automobile, so that was the place I picked. Old-time guide Harry Gaines was recommended, so I picked him.

Little did I realize that I would fall in love with the beautiful river and remain close friends with Gaines until his death in 1991.

A wise-cracking, bearded sourdough character, Gaines was the type of guide who could show you a good time even if you didn't catch a fish. That is the philosophy most guides espouse. They generally do not guarantee fish in the box for the ride home. As more than one guide has said, "That's why they call it fishing, not catching."

Bob Saxton, owner of the Kenai River guide service Silver King Charters, said going out fishing is "enjoying an opportunity not to be at work. Sometimes you even catch a fish. That's the frosting on the cake. We don't really have jobs. When I'm fishing, I'm not working.

"Once I had a group out fishing on a rainy day and someone said, 'You know, Bob, you've got the nicest office I've ever been in. But the roof leaks.'"

Of course every guide talks about providing clients with a good time no matter what, but deep down they really want you to catch a fish in order to be truly fulfilled.

During my visits to the Kenai River, I had many good times with Harry Gaines, but did not catch many fish. In fact, it became a well-publicized joke that I could not catch a king salmon. I was ruining Gaines's reputation.

When Harry was dying, a radio show did a series of reminiscences with him about his years on the river. When asked who was the worst fisherman he ever took out, he didn't hesitate. My name rang out clearly across the air waves.

When I finally did catch a silver salmon with Harry, he got down on his knees in the boat and went through salaam motions.

Everything I know about fishing I learned from Harry Gaines.

(Ha, got you back for that worst fisherman crack, Harry.)

Fact is (notice I didn't say, "True story") I became an Alaska fisherman.

I am now just one of the masses who create traffic jams on the Seward Highway, streaming out of the city in search of a fish-bearing stream.

My growing kinship with Alaska fishermen eventually led me to pen an ode to the species, in the style of "redneck" comedian Jeff Foxworthy and with apologies to him, as well.

Some highlights from "You Might Be a Fisherman . . . "

■ You might be a fisherman if you always thought the guy in *South Pacific* was singing "Salmon Enchanted Evening."

You might be a fisherman if someone tells you to jump in the lake and you wonder if you can catch 'em bare-handed while treading water.

■ You might be a fisherman if you order shrimp cocktail in a restaurant, then shovel the shrimp into a plastic bag for future bait use.

■ It's entirely conceivable you might be a fisherman if you'd rather go fishing than watch the World Series.

You might be a fisherman if you turned down Madonna when she asked to have your child because you had an appointment to dipnet for hooligan.

■ You might be a fisherman if you know flies are meant to be tied, not swatted.

You might be a fisherman if you'd rather watch salmon spawn up close and personal than watch Michelle Pfeiffer and Robert Redford spawn up close and personal.

You might be a fisherman if you cried reading *The Old Man and the Sea* because the guy didn't get to barbecue the fish.

■ There's some likelihood you might be a fisherman if you floss with 20-pound test line.

You might be a fisherman if you hear the words "speed limit" and think of the time your pal Billy Joe Balabushka caught three silvers in fifteen minutes.

You might be a fisherman if your wife drags you to a lecture on foreign cinema and you get misty-eyed when you hear the word "reel."

You might be a fisherman if you hear someone is hooked and your first thought is "Treble?" not "Drugs."

It's possible you might be a fisherman if you think fishing for compliments is what guys in Omaha do who can't get near halibut.

■ You might be a fisherman if the big one that got away in your life was not the girl from Sigma Chi back in college.

You might be a fisherman if it's your dream to someday get the autograph of that guy Evin Rude.

■   And above all, you might be a fisherman if you think the greatest movie of all time is *A River Runs Through It.*

You definitely know someone like this.

This is what Alaskans are like. They work so they can afford to fish. They spend all their summer free time wiggling hooks in the water and all their winter free time dreaming of the next fishing season.

And when they get those opportunities to go out fishing, bizarre things happen. Trust me. These are absolutely, positively true stories.

Lew Freedman

1. Caught Ya!

Somebody forgot to tell John Pezzenti that the idea is to hook the fish.

It was a picturesque day and Pezzenti, a professional wildlife photographer, was making the most of it, enjoying the quiet, the sunlight, on a solitary fishing expedition to the Kenai River. He was not far from Cooper Landing, where he lived at the time.

"It was a perfect Alaska day," he said, recalling the events of the fall of 1989. "It was what dreams are made of."

Or nightmares.

He had just caught and released an 18-inch rainbow trout that seemed longer than his leg. He was astonished to see two huge moose dart out of the trees and splash across the river with two wolves on their trail. Wolves! He couldn't believe it.

Pezzenti was convinced he was fishing in paradise. Until his final cast of the day. He put perhaps a hundred feet of line into the air with a wrist-snapping cast. And promptly hooked himself in the neck. In the jugular vein.

With startling suddenness, the beautiful day turned dangerous. The hook imbedded itself into his flesh and Pezzenti gushed blood. The combination of the force of the hit and the blood pouring out of his body knocked Pezzenti to the ground. He collapsed on the bank at the edge of the water and passed out. He does not know how long he lay unconscious, but when he groggily started to regain his senses, he looked into the face of an older man who said, "That fly needs to come out, son."

No one was in sight when Pezzenti was fishing, but the stranger had apparently been nearby. The man went to his truck and returned with vise grips and a bottle of bourbon as an anesthetic (or so Pezzenti thought). Turns out the booze was for sterilization.

In the end, the man's efforts were only partly successful and he had to drive Pezzenti to the hospital in Seward sixty-five miles away.

"It was scary," said Pezzenti. "I had three feet of line hanging out of my neck and blood all over the front of me."

Such embarrassing and painful incidents occur more often than most fly fishermen would care to admit. Golfers yell, "Fore!" Perhaps fishermen should yell, "Watch out!" Except that frequently they turn out to be the main target, so warnings to the populace at large would be irrelevant.

There should always be someone around to remind careless or plain unlucky fishermen that the object of the game is to hook fish, not commit hara-kiri. However, wherever men travel with implements of destruction there are going to be casualties.

Just ask the folks who staff the emergency room at Central Peninsula Hospital in Soldotna. The medical facility is just a javelin throw or—dare we say it—a long cast from the Kenai River. Thousands of fishermen gather at the river each summer and the law of averages dictates some of them are going to do some harm to themselves. Which is why the hospital began stockpiling flies and hooks and stories, all souvenirs of the crazy things fishermen do to themselves and their friends.

In a typical May-to-August fishing season, doctors at the hospital will remove perhaps two hundred hooks from human flesh. Ouch, ouch, and ouch.

For years now the hospital has saved the hooks as its annual catch, so to speak. For a while, the medical personnel stuck hooks on a felt dummy in the same spots where the hooks were extracted. Then they switched to a felt cloth. Then the plain felt was gussied up and a big, fat, black felt fish hung on a bulletin board near the admitting desk.

The doctors used to save the hooks for a season, then throw them away and start over. In recent years, though, fishermen have been requesting the return of their expensive hooks.

Such terrible things people do to one another.

Once upon a time a man and wife were fishing from the

bank of the Kenai River for red salmon. The woman hooked a fish and began reeling. The fish fought back and so did she. Slowly but surely she brought the fish to land. When victory was declared and the fish was on shore, the man belted the fish with a club to finish it off. Boing! The hook flew out of the fish's mouth, caught on the guy's nose, and parked there.

Next stop, Central Peninsula Hospital.

These weird things happen. They happen a lot. So often that perhaps hooks should be registered at the police station as dangerous weapons.

Rita McNeal, who has managed the emergency room during the high season, said it really isn't that surprising fishermen get pierced by the hooks. They are sharp. And the humans forget they are sharp. The results are messy.

"The intention is to go through the tough skin of the fish and stay there, and it works the same on people," she said.

Generally, the most common injury from the flying hook is a hooked hand. Makes sense since people handle hooks frequently when they're in the boat or on shore, especially if they're baiting the tips. People also get hooked in the head by a neighboring fisherman, especially when they're fishing elbow to elbow.

If a fisherman takes the drastic step of going to the hospital, you can bet that he's really hooked. Hard and deep. Blood is likely to be in the picture. The first inclination upon being hooked is to yank the hook out and pretend the accident never happened. Or work the hook through the flesh and pretend the accident never happened. Usually, this tactic fails and the blood flows more freely. Infection can set in. Most of the time doctors do not recommend treating yourself.

The real question is whether the hooked fisherman is in more pain from the actual penetration of flesh, or from embarrassment. There is definitely a How-Did-This-Happen-To-Me outlook involved.

Bob Stickles of Tri-River Charters in Talkeetna, Alaska, remembers the time one of his assistant guides was fishing for silver salmon in the Susitna River. The guy hooked a fish with a 7/8-ounce green Pixie, but the fish pulled free and that sent the hook airborne. It landed in the guide's nose.

"It was hanging from his bugle," said Stickles. "I give him credit. He took the Pixie off and kept the hook in and finished his charter. He walked into the emergency room with his hand over his face and he said, 'I think it's obvious what I need.'"

Painkillers.

Another visitor to the emergency room was a woman who arrived dressed for an evening out, but sporting a hook in her cheek. One guy hooked his baseball cap to his scalp. The hook, the hat, and the hair all combined to produce a big, tangled mess.

Kenai River guide Reuben Hanke has a doozy of a tale. He was guiding a group of king salmon fishermen and one client caught a fish. Before the fish was subdued it swam under the boat. Hanke was watching for its re-emergence when he heard a shout behind him. He spun around and there was the fish. The king had jumped into the boat and landed on another fisherman's lap.

The fish squirmed, flopped, shook its head, and the hook popped free. People were hopping around, the fish was clubbed, and everyone calmed down. But the man whose lap had acted as a baseball glove motioned to Hanke. When Hanke bent over, the man whispered, "Can you get the hook out of my butt?"

"So we had to perform surgery in the boat," said Hanke.

Such impromptu action by guides probably outnumbers by a wide margin the number of times trained medical professionals get involved in pain-relieving activity. For one thing, often the body-piercing occurs far, far from a hospital. Other times the shock of the hit is the worst injury suffered. Not to mention the blushing. Who wants it broadcast on the six o'clock news that you've botched a cast and instead of catching a fish caught a person?

Gary Galbraith, a guide on the upper Kenai River, once brought a client to a little island in the middle of the river to fish for rainbow trout and red salmon. The man was standing in some brush casting into the water. His wife stood nearby, facing the other way. Zip goes the line through the air. Pow goes the hook as it imbeds itself in the lady's head.

"He catches his wife," said Galbraith.

Right in the noggin. She had no idea what happened, just felt the sting on her head. She panicked and began running around. The man was far enough away that he thought he had a big fish on the line.

"She thought she had something in her hair, like a bee stinging her," said Galbraith. "But he's all excited."

It didn't take long for the man's emotional high to dissipate, though, when the sounds of his wife screaming drowned out everything around. In this case the hook was removed on the spot. "It didn't take long," said Galbraith, "but it seems like an eternity, even if it's only fifteen seconds."

It was not clear if it took more than fifteen seconds for the woman to begin speaking to the fisherman again, however.

And then there was the one about beginner's bad luck. The story goes that a secretary at the University of Alaska Anchorage went fly-fishing with some friends for the very first time.

She made a cast and sure enough, right away she hooked herself in the back of the head.

The hook was carefully removed by her partners and, undaunted by this somewhat uneasy introduction to the sport, she readied herself, cast out again—and hooked herself all over again!

After the hook was once again laboriously and carefully removed from her body, she shouted, "I'm not giving up!"

Maybe not, but no one would stand very close to her, either.

That woman had an impressive attitude, but there are times when a hook hooking in the wrong place produces excruciating circumstances. It's hard to top the tale told by guide Dale Benson, who once took a couple from Anchorage fly-fishing for kings a hundred or so miles away at Lake Creek. The man was the far more serious fisherman.

While the man cast again and again, the woman, who was attractive and about thirty-five years old, took breaks frequently and roamed up and down the shore, gazing at the flowers, enjoying the setting.

On one cast the man ripped back very hard and with wonderful, crisp form brought his rod forward and propelled his fly ahead. Naturally, he caught his wife. The hook pierced her thin jacket, her shirt, and her bra, and lodged in the nipple of her breast.

"Boy, did she howl," said Benson.

The woman was bleeding all over the place, right through all those layers. Abruptly, from a peaceful, idyllic trip, they had shifted to a war zone.

After the initial shock, the woman tried to remove the hook through her clothes. Then the man tried to help her. It was an awkward scene given the delicacy of the situation and the location of the wound. But nothing was working. The hook was stuck but good.

Finally, the woman said the hell with modesty—cut the bra off and get the hook out of her. Clothes were peeled back and Benson threaded the hook the rest of the way through her nipple by using a pair of pliers.

That wound probably smarted for a long while. The woman likely soon took up a safer hobby, like wrestling alligators.

2. Paradise Won and Paradise Lost

"You can tell a fisherman's lying if his lips are moving." Great saying, huh?

Those are the words of Alaskan fisherman and fishing guide Gary Galbraith, who in the next sentence boasts of how he caught a limit of three Kenai River red salmon with a single cast.

"I've caught three fish in one cast," said Galbraith. "Three reds on a stringer. I felt the tug and I thought, 'Wow, that's a big one.' I had my limit. They were all hooked in the mouth."

Well, you can't say he didn't warn you.

Galbraith lives in Cooper Landing, which is a small town located about a hundred miles from Anchorage on the Kenai Peninsula.

Although most of his fishing time is spent on the Kenai River, what sets Galbraith apart from the typical Kenai fishing guide and king salmon chaser is that he fishes in the upper part of the river.

According to Alaska state fish and game biologist Dave Nelson, the Kenai River is eighty-two miles long, originating in Kenai Lake and running to Cook Inlet. From Kenai Lake, which is in Cooper Landing, it passes through Skilak Lake and runs under the Soldotna Bridge. That fifty miles is generally considered the upper river, and the most heavily fished stretch of the upper river is concentrated around Cooper Landing.

The upper Kenai River is closed to motorboat transport. Which means most of Galbraith's fishing is done from a rubber raft propelled downstream by human power, usually the power residing in his shoulders. Of course, many times the raft unloads its occupants on the bank, too. But overall, this is a very different type of fishery than the happy hunting grounds of the lower Kenai River, where guides and clients cover dozens of miles in one trip.

"Fishing from a raft is better than from a drift boat," said Galbraith. "It's quiet. It's safe. It doesn't tip over. It's a completely different technique. You get one shot at it basically."

In other words, when you're floating by. You can't rev up the engine and retrace your steps to try the same fishing hole repeatedly.

In his two decades of upper Kenai fishing, Galbraith's clients have caught nine kinds of fish—four species of salmon, rainbow trout, Dolly Varden, grayling, whitefish, and lake trout.

Galbraith lives in a handmade log cabin he built himself, and with the river out his back door, he figures he lives in a paradise. However, things do go haywire in paradise, just as they do anywhere fishermen congregate. And being a guide you maximize your chances for the bizarre to come calling.

About ten years ago, Galbraith had three women from Tennessee fishing with him. They were all in their sixties, but they were fun-loving, not too staid. He steered his raft to the shore of an island for a break, planning to serve a snack. As long as they were parking their river-going vessel, one of the women said she should go to the bathroom.

"There are the bushes," said Galbraith.

No problem. The woman discreetly stepped out of sight, into the brush, dropped her trousers, and relieved herself. Just as she pulled up her pants, she let out a squeal and came running out of the trees.

Was there a bear chasing her? Some other wild animal? Sort of. There was a man lying in the brush.

Turns out, it was a state fish and game agent trying to be invisible. He was wearing a camouflage outfit and was in position to spy on fishermen flouting the law. He didn't want to blow his cover, and when the woman squatted just about on top of him, he figured the best thing to do was stay quiet and out of sight.

"She tinkled pretty near right on him," said Galbraith. "He was so embarrassed, he didn't move."

Until she screamed.

That was the end of the man toughing it out. The guy stood up and sheepishly said, "Hi, Gary."

The woman had a pretty good attitude about the entire mix-up. As they packed up the raft and headed back out on the river, she said, "That poor young man will never be the same. He saw things he'll never get over."

A year later, Galbraith brought a different load of people to the same island for a routine snack and break. That time Galbraith actually spotted the same agent lying in the bushes and casually announced loudly to the group that he had to go to the bathroom. Galbraith began walking right to the spot where the man was hidden. No trying to lay low this time. He popped up and said to Galbraith, "Don't even think about it."

Wonder what the charges would have read like if Galbraith had proceeded to take care of business.

Once Galbraith had eight Japanese middle-aged men and women fishing with him and not one of them spoke a word of English.

"It was hard making them realize what they had to do," said Galbraith.

Understandable. But they did know they wanted some fish.

"The leader of the group hooked into a big Dolly Varden," said Galbraith. "It was maybe 24 inches long, weighing about five pounds. We're getting it up to the boat, getting it up. I had the net ready. I was just ready to scoop it out of the water and they're all standing up in the boat clapping. But then the guy who had the fish on his line started clapping, too."

Clapping, of course, involves two hands. So the fisherman promptly dropped the rod over the side.

"They all just sat down and didn't say a word."

Galbraith has had plenty of experience with fishing rods diving overboard.

He also guides for halibut in Resurrection Bay in Seward, using a much larger boat. Once, after a nice fishing catch, it was time to pack up for the day and head back to land. Galbraith was at the wheel. He yelled to the fishermen to park their rods on the cabin roof.

"They just laid them on the top," said Galbraith. "Then we hit some big swells."

Bye-bye fishing poles. His own fault for not checking to see if the rods were secured, said Galbraith.

"They're just in 450 feet of water," he said.

That's one thing about fishing in the ocean. It's a long way down. Not that it's easy to find a fishing rod that's gone swimming in the six-foot-deep Kenai River, either.

Once, a client fishing with Galbraith on the upper Kenai brought along a brand-new, fancy $600 rod. You wouldn't know it was any kind of prized possession, though, by the careless way he treated it.

"We were drifting down the river and I said, 'You'd better hold on to that,'" said Galbraith. "It doesn't take much to take a rod out of the boat."

The man said he was fine, not to worry, that he had his eye on the rod. Turns out his eye was all he had on it, not his hand. Not ten seconds after Galbraith's warning, a fish took the bait and there went the rod into the river. Gone. The fisherman was in absolute shock.

"The rod was a birthday present from his wife," said Galbraith. "He spent the rest of the trip trying to decide if he had enough room left on his credit card to buy another one. It had to be replaced."

Galbraith chose not to say, "I told you so."

There have been times, however, when Galbraith refused to give fishermen any slack. The know-it-alls who refuse to listen and act rudely are the ones he likes to give some payback.

"I like to win money fishing," said Galbraith.

About eight years ago, Galbraith had a quartet of anglers from the state of Washington out fishing.

"They are all pros, all know exactly what they're doing, and they don't think they need to listen to the guide," said Galbraith.

Wrong approach. Each fishing hole, each fishing area, in Alaska or indeed anywhere in the country, has its own peculiarities. Without a bit of luck, it takes some local wisdom to find the fish.

"I was trying to explain to them how to fish the river," said Galbraith. "I said, 'It's not going to happen unless you do what I say.'"

One of the fishermen, who was not inclined to listen, kept

casting his line in the water without anything happening, and he said Galbraith didn't know his butt from a hole in the ground.

"He was lucky I didn't clobber him," said Galbraith.

Instead of throwing a left hook, Galbraith parked the raft at a nearby bank, pulled out a dilapidated old fishing rod, and challenged the man a different way.

"I said, 'See this piece of junk? I bet you twenty bucks that in one cast I get one fish,'" said Galbraith.

The man took the bet.

Galbraith reared back, cast, and Boom! he caught a fish. Right away. One cast, one fish. He stared at the other angler and said, "Want me to do it again?"

Another twenty-dollar bet. Another cast, another fish.

"We can keep going if you want," Galbraith said to the grumpy man.

"By the time I was finished, I had eighty dollars."

And a greatly subdued fisherman. Four casts, four fish. Galbraith stood with his hand out, waiting to be paid on the spot.

"I wanted to see the flash," said Galbraith.

The only response the man could muster was a low-grade grumble: "I knew there were fish in there."

Fish he might have caught if he'd been paying attention in class.

3. Chasing the Kenai King

Most anglers who fish the Kenai River are after salmon. But Chuck Tozer had an even bigger catch in mind.

In the summer of 1994, Tozer, an Anchorage sports broadcaster and businessman, hatched a scheme with his favorite guide, Mike Fenton. He showed up with his girlfriend Sue, ostensibly to catch fish.

They had been fishing on the river for some time when opportunity arose. Sue was taking a bathroom break. With Fenton's complicity, Tozer tied an engagement ring on the end of his lure. It was some ring, a sapphire surrounded by twelve diamonds. Who wouldn't take the bait?

Sue returned from her intermission and Fenton played his acting role, handing her the rod and telling her to crank the reel five revolutions in order to drop the hook to the bottom of the river.

But worried that the ring would slip off, Fenton changed his mind and cut the scene short. After Sue barely began letting her line out, he ad-libbed, "Hey, you've got a snag."

So Sue reeled in and Fenton examined the end of the hook. In mock surprise he said, "Hey, what's this?" The shiny object glistened in the light.

Even without rehearsal, Sue played her designated role perfectly, shouting, "There's a ring on there!"

Then Tozer proposed and Sue accepted.

"It was really romantic," said Tozer.

The Kenai Peninsula features some of the most fabulous fishing in the world, and the Kenai River itself is world-renowned for the pursuit of king salmon, red salmon, and silver salmon.

Its green waters are fed by glacial melt, which keeps the water murky. You cannot see fish beneath the surface on the Kenai, even if they are right next to your boat. The river flows at about six miles an hour, and it is usually only about six feet deep at its deepest points.

Of the several types of salmon, spawning king salmon are the first to return to the river each spring, usually by mid-May, and after winter's comparative dormancy, their arrival ignites a special spark in the Alaskan angler. Fishermen are itching to get out of the house, get out of town, and go fishing, and the king is usually the first fish to chase each year. "The kings are in!" go the announcements heralding the return of the big fish. It is reminiscent of the word-of-mouth shouts that "The British are coming" from the Revolutionary War.

King salmon have a special mystique in Alaska. Although salmon is a popular fixture on the menus of the best restaurants, nonetheless with a subsistence-oriented, he-man provider outlook, Alaska fishermen pride themselves on filling their own freezers with salmon steaks.

Yet that is easier said than done. Salmon are a prized catch. State fish and game officials estimate it takes an angler upward of twenty-four hours of fishing time to catch one king.

Once hooked, the king salmon also can be a hard-fighting fish. A keeper from the Kenai River will weigh at least 30 pounds, but the world-record king salmon, caught by a sport fisherman in this very area, weighed 97¼ pounds.

Joe Hanes, a Kenai River guide for two decades, said the biggest king ever caught with him weighed 78 pounds. Sounds gigantic, but he isn't satisfied.

"It's unbelievable that all the time I've been chasing them I haven't got one over 80," he said. "I'm due."

Due because Hanes remains optimistic that the mythic 100-pound king salmon is out there, waiting to make some fisherman and fishing guide famous throughout Alaska and throughout the sport.

The idea that a world record might be hooked with the next cast is a powerful lure for thousands of fishermen who come not only from all parts of Alaska in abundance, but from all over the world.

And where fishermen congregate, things are bound to happen.

Al Grillo, an Anchorage photographer, fishes whenever he can during the summer months. Once, in the early 1990s, he was out fishing with his wife, Brenda, and she hooked into a king salmon. This was her very first king.

"She was fighting the fish and a can of 7-Up came floating by," said Grillo.

The can captured her attention and as it bobbed along she reached out to grab it.

"I say, 'What are you doing?'" said Grillo.

After all, 7-Up is available at any convenience store, and a king salmon might decide to attach itself to your hook only once a year.

Grillo told Brenda to ignore the soda, but she didn't heed him. With one hand she held the rod, and with the other she scooped up the can, which was full. Then she promptly reeled in the fish.

"She caught a 50-pound king and a twelve-ounce 7-Up," said Grillo.

Happy ending. As it was for Grillo's friend Doug Van Reeth, a former Alaskan photographer. Grillo, Van Reeth, and another friend from Florida were also fishing on the Kenai River. The men were just enjoying the day, figuring if they caught something sizable it would be a nice bonus.

All of a sudden, Van Reeth's pole bent just about double. Either Moby Dick was on the other end, or he had snagged an impressive log.

"Got the bottom, Doug?" Van Reeth was teased.

Calm, unruffled, showing no excitement, Van Reeth said, "No, I've got a fish."

What a fish it was. No doubt a distant cousin of Moby Dick, the king weighed 75 pounds.

Sounds like the thing to do is go fishing with Al Grillo and you'll catch a suitcase-sized king salmon, right?

Nope.

"I'll tell you a story that will break your heart," said Grillo.

Which sounds suspiciously like a euphemism for "True story."

This time Al himself was the one with the fishing pole in his hands. A Kenai king took his bait and chomped the line but good.

"I hooked into this big sucker," said Grillo. "It just fights like a son of a bitch, jumping out of the water and skimming across the surface. It did this three or four times. People in other boats are videotaping."

Grillo waged a fifteen-minute battle before reeling the fish up to the boat.

"I get it right by the boat and it takes off again," he said. "Then it turns on its side. It's tired."

Grillo was very excited, convinced he had a 70-pound king salmon surrendering. The net was lowered and the fish scooped into the net.

"I pulled the back end of the fish up and it's halfway into the boat," said Grillo.

Only suddenly, the fish was gone. Now you see it, now you don't. No weight in the net. Vanished into thin air. Grillo stared at the net and was stunned to see a hole in the mesh. And the hole was six inches wide. When he held it up in the air to examine it more closely, everyone fishing around him saw it too.

"There was an audible sigh," said Grillo. "There was a loud 'Ohh.' Everybody on the river felt the disappointment. I have a picture of the hole in the net."

This incident occurred a few years ago, and as proof of "The Big One That Got Away Syndrome," Grillo now says of the salmon escapee, "It had to be 100 pounds."

The fish is like Pinocchio's nose. It keeps growing.

It was poet Robert W. Service who referred to the strange things that happen in the land of the midnight sun. He wasn't talking about fishing, but he could have been.

Guide Reuben Hanke, who has operated Harry Gaines Fishing since Gaines's death in 1991, said he is almost ashamed to admit that the largest king salmon he has caught himself weighed just 64 pounds.

"That ain't fair," said Hanke.

Of course, there are mitigating circumstances. Guides have little time to fish for kings themselves. They're too busy showing other anglers how to find fish, how to bring them in, and then how to find some more fish, though there is a limit of one king salmon per day, per fisherman, on the Kenai River.

The largest king caught in a Hanke boat does far exceed his personal catch, weighing 84 pounds. An 84-pound king salmon might outweigh a fifth-grader and be as tall, so while it's shy of the 1985 world record caught by Soldotna's Les Anderson, that's a significant haul and if you are one to boast, it's something worth boasting about.

If all his years guiding on the river have made Hanke as much of an expert on king salmon behavior as a member of another species can be, it has also made him a student of human behavior. As he puts it, of the anglers who walk up to his guide service asking to be taken fishing for five or six hours at a crack, "I can't predict what people are going to do."

Take the time a couple in their seventies and a similarly aged friend traveled to Alaska in a motor home from the Lower 48 during a catch-and-release period on the Kenai.

There are years when king salmon are bountiful, and there are years when the crop is lean. When it seems that fewer king salmon are returning to the river than it might take to keep the species thriving, state fish and game agents step in to regulate the fishery. Limits may be reduced in some cases and in some places, or in the interests of conservation, all fishing may be halted except for catch-and-release. That means an angler may still hook a big fish, but won't be able to take it home.

Some anglers don't bother to fish when this happens, but others are perfectly content to fish for the fun and experience. When this elderly trio showed up, Hanke carefully explained the rules. You can catch fish, but you have to put them back in the river. Are you sure you want go to? he asked them.

They understood the law, they said, and they wanted to go.

The two men sat in the front seats of the twenty-foot boat near Hanke's steering seat and the woman sat in the rear of the boat. They were trolling in the well-known Big Eddy fishing hole and it was warm and sunny.

"I was doing a lot of talking because I was afraid these guys were going to fall asleep, get a bite, and lose the rods," said Hanke.

In mid-sentence, however, Hanke noticed the woman stand up. She was backing toward the middle of the boat, claiming she had a snag and was trying to shake the hook loose. Her rod was bent in an arc. No snag, she had a fish.

Pandemonium. The woman was staggering all over the boat, the fish was pulling, and her husband was jealous. He wanted to catch the fish.

"The old boy wanted the rod from her," said Hanke. "And she wouldn't give it to him."

The struggle (between woman and fish) continued for about twenty-five minutes and after the exhausting tug-of-war, the king was reeled to the side of the boat. As the fish nestled into the net, Hanke estimated its weight at 75 pounds.

Hanke had the woman hold the metal-handled net as he leaned over the side to remove the hook from the fish's mouth. He then held the fish under the water, made sure it revived, and set it free. But when he straightened up minus the fish, the woman went berserk.

"She went nuts and started hitting me with the net," said Hanke. "I couldn't believe it. I thought she was going to run me out of the boat. She was livid. Believe me, there ain't much room to get away. It was wild."

Both guys were mad because they didn't catch anything. The husband was mad because she didn't let him bring in her fish. And she was mad because she didn't get to keep the fish. But she knew the rule going in—catch and release.

Although this account proves that having English as a native tongue doesn't necessarily ensure communication, Kenai River guide Raymond McGuire recalls a trying trip for a different reason—everyone on the boat except him spoke only Japanese.

"A couple of them let all the line out, just emptied the spool," said McGuire. "It was a hard time trying to communicate."

One angler hooked a fish and the other three fishermen dutifully laid their rods down so there would be no accidental entanglement. However, they laid their rods hanging over the edge of the boat, so the lines still dangled. While one angler jumped up and down yelling and snapping pictures, the fisherman got the fish all tied up with two other lines.

"It just didn't work for him," said McGuire.

You never know what to expect on the Kenai River. Ask guide David Zaboroskie.

"The biggest surprise of my life was to find myself in the river," he said.

Someone in the boat caught a line in the boat's propeller. No movement until the line was freed.

Zaboroskie was leaning over the rear of the boat working to cut the line loose, and the next thing he knew he was swimming in the Kenai. He fell forward, head first, into the water.

Another time, Zaboroskie had his boat parked in a hot fishing spot, teaching someone how to back-troll. In back-trolling, the engine is running, and the boat is not anchored, but moves very slowly and gradually away from a prime spot. When a fisherman hooks into a king, the boat can be used to help set the hook by giving the engine a sudden boost.

An angler in the boat yelled, "Got one!" Zaboroskie hit the engine, but the rod sailed forward, out of the man's hands. In a brilliant fielding play worthy of an all-star shortstop, Zaboroskie lunged forward and grabbed the rod before it disappeared, but in so doing, was thrown off-balance. As if in a Keystone Kops routine, he stumbled into the engine throttle, the boat took off, and simultaneously the rod came apart in his hands.

It only took seconds, but Zaboroskie got the boat under control, and with the fish still hooked, circled the king until the rod could be repaired. Somehow, the fish stayed on the line, the rod was fixed, and the fish was reeled in.

Victory.

"A lot of people were standing around watching that one," said Zaboroskie.

Normally, a guide prefers to keep such a story quiet, or to tell it on his own terms. But there were many witnesses. Zaboroskie was fortunate that the comical event turned out well.

That was a story a guide could be proud of, but sometimes a guide is embarrassed by what happens and doesn't want to ever see his name attached to the occurrence. Which explains the anonymous nature of another tale.

A beginning guide had four clients out on one of his first-ever king salmon fishing trips on the Kenai River and it seemed all four lines tangled at the same time when one angler hooked into a fish. The guide had everybody stop what they were doing. He took out a sharp utensil and snipped one line, believing he had solved the mess with minimal hassle.

In the movies, when a line is cut like that it usually involves a bomb. The under-pressure, sweating hero has to choose between the red wire and the blue wire, always chooses correctly, and everyone is saved. Well, in this case, if our intrepid guide was defusing a bomb, there would have been massive casualties.

It turned out that particular line wasn't tangled up with the others at all. In fact all the snip accomplished was setting the fish free. In the words of Desi Arnaz to his screwball wife Lucille Ball, "Lucy, you've got some 'splainin' to do."

Actually, there's no explaining many things that happen on the Kenai River. There's definitely no logical way to explain the fish. Guides know that the fish normally come in on the high tide. They know where the best fishing holes are and they know that the fish tend to hug the contours of the banks or the sandbars.

Past experience is the educator here, but even knowing all of that stuff doesn't mean you can find fish when you want them. The fish do what the fish do, and the wise fisherman considers himself lucky when their paths intersect.

Joe Connors, who operates Big Sky Charter and Fish Camp in Sterling, has guided on the Kenai Peninsula for a quarter century, and with a biggest-ever catch of 94 pounds, he thinks he knows what he's doing and where the kings are.

One day during the summer of 1996, Connors had a handful of people out fishing with him. They're sitting in the boat and nothing is happening. Then one of the clients says, "Why are those fish swimming over there?"

Connors looks up and a short distance away sees a king jumping out of what might have been six inches of water next to a gravel bar. So he motors over and starts fishing in the spot. Immediately, two anglers catch kings at the same time. Then another boat of Connors's clients, led by an assistant guide, comes over.

"There's fish in this one hole," said Connors.

One of the clients was a man with only one arm. He caught

a 35-pound king, but inspired by the activity and the size of fish others caught, he released what normally would be a keeper. He said he had to have a bigger fish.

"Sure enough, he hooks into another fish," said Connors. "A 71-pounder. He was yelling at the top of his lungs. It was one hell of a day. We got three that were 70-pounders."

The odds of catching three 70-pounders in the same area, on the same trip, on the same day, are probably only slightly better than winning the big prize in the New York State Lottery.

But here's the punch line: Connors returned to the same fishing hole for the rest of the summer and caught just one more fish.

Connors said he was thrilled for the one-armed man and that he gets great pleasure out of making anglers happy, especially if they have special circumstances. He saves photos from his trips and keeps them in scrapbooks, and some of those pictures warm his heart.

Not long ago, Connors had a client fishing who at age two had been burned over 90 percent of his body. When he came fishing with his dad and grandfather, the young man was then eighteen years old. He was so badly burned he had only stubs for hands, but on the first day of the trip he caught a 35-pound king salmon.

The next day, said Connors, the young man boasted he was going to catch an even bigger fish.

"He bet with his dad that he would," said Connors. "He hooked into another fish and he fought it all by himself. I'd lift the rod up and he'd reel. When we brought it in it was a 60-pound fish. I thought what he did was beautiful."

4. If You Think Salmon Come Easy, Buy Some in a Can

One day in the summer of 1995, fishing guide Reuben Hanke was idly casting from the bank on his property along the Kenai River when he hooked into a red salmon.

Rather than immediately reel in the fish, which weighed between eight and ten pounds, Hanke handed the rod to his three-year-old daughter, Rachel. Daddy's girl was ready and willing to take her first fish. After watching all the people come and go and catch fish right there at her home her whole life, she wanted one of her very own.

"It was probably the most intense tug-of-war I've ever seen," said Hanke. "She grabbed the rod, but she couldn't reel it."

Rachel weighed perhaps thirty pounds and was only a few feet tall. Initially, she rested the pole against her belly, in the same manner she had seen other anglers do it.

"She's trying to do it like the pros," said Hanke, "but I told her to turn around and put it over her shoulder. That's when the war started."

Picture the scene: This little tyke straining and pulling and marching forward with a fishing pole over one shoulder as a fish strains and pulls on the other end. This went on for about ten minutes.

"She landed it," said Hanke, who was laughing so hard, he said, "I almost busted a gut. She couldn't get me after it with a bat fast enough. She was screaming at the top of her lungs, 'Don't let it get away!'"

The fish was taken, cleaned, and brought into the house.

"We had to eat it that night," said Hanke. "She felt she was pulling her weight feeding the family. I just couldn't believe I didn't have a video camera going. She's gonna be an Alaska gal."

That's the way Mike Turner felt when he took his daughter Sara on her first boat ride in an inflatable raft on the Kenai when she was about eight years old. She was really frightened and had no interest in fishing at first, he recalled nine years later.

"Oh, Dad," Turner remembered her saying, "the salmon will pull me out of the boat."

Turner assured Sara that wouldn't happen.

"I had to negotiate just to get her to let go of the side of the boat," said Turner. "It took a lot of coaxing."

Five minutes into the drift, Sara hooked a fish.

"She was not about to let go of that rod," said Turner. "She was real excited. A friend held on to her as she fought it. She weighed 58 pounds at the time and the fish weighed 61. She became a fisherwoman then. That's as good as it gets. I was a proud papa."

In the years since, he said, Sara has become quite an accomplished angler.

"She's very, very good," said Turner. "She always gets one in about ten minutes. She releases 40- to 60-pounders."

Some people have the touch and some people are lucky. And some people have both. Of course, there's luck and there's luck.

Long-time Kenai River salmon guide Rod Berg said perhaps the most amazing thing he's seen on the river occurred about three years ago in a one-week period. He was fishing on Beaver Creek on the lower Kenai when he watched a fisherman hook a 40-pound king that made a short run—and then leapt right into the boat.

"There was a real crowd around," said Berg. "Everyone stood up and started clapping."

Later in the week, fishing nearby, Berg saw another angler hook a fish for the same guide only to have the fish launch itself into the air, not once, not twice, but three times. On the third jump the fish landed right in the boat. Instant replay.

"That's a fish from heaven," said Berg. "It wasn't landed, it landed itself. Everyone was shaking their heads."

Who said fish can't fly?

A couple of years later, Berg said a king that he guessed weighed 50 pounds shot out of the water like a torpedo and made for his boat.

"It balanced on the gunnel of the boat for a second," said Berg. "It was teetering and flopping."

But it didn't actually make it over the side.

Another time fishing on the Kenai, one of his clients hooked a king and was playing it when a lead weight dropped overboard. The weight caught on a rod lying on the track unused and pulled the $250 item into the water, where it disappeared. An hour later, Berg got a call on the radio from one of his fishing partners in another boat.

"He said, 'Hey, Rod, I got your rod back,'" said Berg.

A pretty good catch.

Co-guide Randy Berg said in his eighteen seasons on the river, the largest king he's caught hit the scales at a fraction under 90 pounds. Bringing in a fish that large is a thrill, said Berg, but most of the time you don't realize how large the king is until it's landed.

"A 40-pounder can take off like an 80-pounder, so we didn't know," said Randy Berg. "It took ten minutes before we realized how big it was and a half-hour to get it in. The fisherman fought it well.

"When you see one that big you hear your heart beat. Those are the ones you know the hook's going to fly out of any second. Big ones seem to get away more often. They don't get that big by being stupid. One thing I learned a long time ago is that they ain't there until they're in the net. I've lost three big fish at the net over the years."

Usually, the fish gets away because the angler is too excited and won't keep the rod tip down far enough, said Berg.

"I just shake my head because I know it's going to be my fault in their minds for the rest of their lives," he said.

The man sounds like a serious philosopher and just maybe all fishing guides become philosophical. Certainly Bob Saxton

of Silver King Charters can make Aristotle sound like a dilet-
tante at times. Saxton defines a bad fishing day as a day when
everyone else is catching fish and he's not.

"I take it a little personal," said Saxton, who is a great believer in anglers having a good time. "It's the bite and the fight.
We might tell a story or two, but we never lie. I only take kids
fishing. Some of them are in their eighties."

Saxton began guiding on the Kenai River part-time in 1973
and full-time in 1978. His change came abruptly. He was working as an insurance company manager when he went down to
the river. He was supposed to return to Anchorage for a man-
datory meeting the next day, but didn't. Instead, he bought a
piece of property and set up shop on the river. As for his insurance career, Saxton says, "I've taken a leave of absence since
1978."

Among Saxton's favorite clients are a couple from Hawaii,
who came around about six years ago and said they wanted to
go fishing for silver salmon. One problem: They showed up
wearing tank tops, shorts, and thongs, and it was September in
Alaska, when temperatures can reasonably be expected to dip
into the thirties. Especially when it's wet outside.

"They didn't have any idea what to bring," said Saxton.

It was raining and cold when the couple appeared and
Saxton would have had to take them both to the hospital for
hypothermia treatment if he didn't provide rain gear and boots.
But the fish were hopping that day, and the visitors had such a
good time they now come year after year.

After their first experience, the anglers went shopping,
bought wool shirts, long johns, and insulated boots, and stored
it all in a duffel bag with Saxton.

"They have no need for the clothes any other time," he said.

Years ago, Saxton watched an angler in a nearby boat have
a salmon hit his rod and send the rod overboard.

"Then he sits back like Mr. Cool," said Saxton. "Like, 'It
wasn't me.'"

Soon after, a fisherman in Saxton's boat hooked a salmon
and when he reeled it in it was attached to another rod.

"We yell over to the other boat, 'This your rod?'" said Saxton. "He goes, 'Uh-huh.' 'Suppose you want the fish, too?' 'Uh-huh.' 'We'll trade you for a beer.'"

Once Saxton had two Japanese couples fishing for kings who said they needed a pit stop.

"We pulled over to shore and the gals climbed up a slick, muddy bank and went into the woods," said Saxton. "After a few minutes we heard a scream. One lady came running out of the trees and slid down the bank. We asked what was wrong. She's going, 'Bear, bear, bear.'"

Before anyone could react, a small Black Angus calf walked out of the woods.

The men teased the woman mercilessly and there was much talk about Alaska wildlife, ranging from bears to moose to caribou. As the second woman reappeared, the first woman, quite angry about her verbal mistreatment, responded by saying, "If you think that's so funny, you should have seen her trying to climb a tree with her pants down."

As many novices as experts fish for king salmon. Many don't know the rules of the river, the laws of the land, or the protocol of fishing. Guides generally provide the appropriate gear to give a beginner a fighting chance to win any match-up with a salmon, but some fishermen prefer unusual challenges.

Ken Robertson of Alaska Drift Boaters operates a business which takes people on the Kenai River without motorized transport. Some of them just like to ride for fun, and he rows, rows, rows the boat. But he also has had some people fish for kings with fly rod equipment. The two don't go together.

Normally, a king salmon would be too strong for the gear and would just break free easily and escape, or break the rod. Yet astonishingly, Robertson caught a 73-pound king on a fly rod.

"I'm the only one I know of who does that with a single action reel," said Robertson. "I get people who like to do that."

Veteran Kenai guide Hanke characterized Robertson's big catch as "an amazing feat. That means all the power comes from the person."

More commonly, a 40-pound test line would be used for big

king salmon, but accidents do happen. Mike Fenton of the Fenton Brothers guide service set a world record without planning to do so on July 31, 1986. He caught a 67¼-pound king salmon on 12-pound test line.

This was Fenton's first year of guiding, and it was the last day of the king salmon season on the Kenai River. A boat load of clients limited out and cut short its trip, so Fenton was hanging around, killing time. Fishing from shore, he made some casts. Fenton hooked one fish and lost it, but when he hooked another the hook stuck.

"There was a little raft nearby and I jumped into it," said Fenton. "I fought it for about fifteen minutes. It circled under the boat and then it swam right into the net. I had no intention of getting any line class record. The only reason I even kept it was because it was the last day of the season."

Fenton was awarded a nice certificate, which he framed, and eleven years later his catch was still a record. He likes to joke that he can make a living off his appearance fees at autograph parties.

Someone who really does sign a lot of autographs is ninety-two-year-old Alaskan adventurer and author Norman Vaughan. Well-known for his travels in the Iditarod Trail Sled Dog Race, as well as for climbing a 10,000-foot mountain named for him in Antarctica, Vaughan took a Kenai River fishing trip in the summer of 1997 and caught the king salmon of his dreams. Or rather, he caught a king salmon in his dreams.

This is what happened. Vaughan and his wife Carolyn drove from Anchorage to Kenai during the night and hooked up with a guide about 4 A.M. So the trip on the river began on no sleep.

As time passed, Vaughan dozed off in the boat, which is why he classified his efforts as "lazy man's fishing." Vaughan was sound asleep, rod by his side, when he got a bite.

"All of a sudden, I was jerked awake by the guide's giving full throttle to the outboard," said Vaughan. "He had seen my fishing pole bend down into a veritable 'U.' I didn't know what was going on. He set the hook by this sudden jerk forward." Soon Vaughan was wide awake and he fought the fish for the next twenty minutes. He brought in a 51-pound king salmon and it was soon cremated for dinner.

"It was wonderful," said Vaughan. "It even tasted better than salmon other people caught."

Vaughan had the fish weighed and measured, and when he got home he had matting board cut in the same size and shape as the fish (ensuring, he noted, that it would never grow in exaggeration). He now uses the board to lean on when he writes letters.

"It was a good, long fish," said Vaughan. "It would extend over a man's normal desk. I think that's a good fishing story because it's not a lie."

The truth will set any fisherman free.

5. What Are the Odds?

The seven-year-old girl from Portland, Oregon, was a lucky kid, guide Joe Hanes figured. She hooked into a 55-pound king salmon and worked it like a pro. She reeled and reeled and had the big fish right up next to the boat.

Hanes was poised to net it, but suddenly the fish spit the hook and swam off, leaving everyone startled and depressed.

"I was thinking, 'Boy, it's going to be hard to get another one,'" said Hanes, a Kenai River guide for the last two decades.

Hopeless case, right? Nope. The little girl hooked another king salmon. Another big one. She reeled and reeled again. By herself. With the only help coming from Hanes holding the rod up.

This fish stayed hooked and was hauled into the boat. It weighed 52 pounds, and the excited kid, no doubt influenced by her movie-watching, proclaimed it "The Lion King, The King of Kings."

Maybe Hanes is the one who is just a lucky guy, because when he's involved in a situation, things seem to work out for the best.

About ten years ago Hanes had a Minnesota gentleman fishing the Kenai with him. The man was eighty-six years old, and this was likely to be the only opportunity of his life to catch a king.

It was the height of the fishing season, a Saturday in July, when the man hooked a fish.

"I'm really trying to help this guy and make sure he doesn't have a heart attack," said Hanes.

All of a sudden from behind him, though, Hanes heard a

shout. Another man was yelling at them. "Hey, hey!" he said. "What are you doing? That's my fish!"

Hanes spun around and saw a guy fishing nearby in a rubber raft with the fish in question lying on its side between the raft and the boat. Apparently, the fish had rolled over the two lines and they had gotten crossed. The hook from Hanes's client was in the right side of the fish's mouth, and the hook from the other guy's rod was imbedded in the left side of the fish's mouth.

"This is a problem," said Hanes.

The wisdom of Solomon was called for. Perhaps the fish could be cut in half?

"We never argued that," said Hanes, who decided there was only one logical way to solve this.

"I said, 'I'll flip a coin and you call it in the air.'"

The guy in the rubber raft won, took the fish, and moved away along the river. Hanes tried to shrug it off as a that's-the-way-it-goes circumstance. It was clear to him, though, that the old man was heartbroken, even if he wasn't complaining.

They resumed fishing, but about a half-hour later, who should appear but the fisherman in the rubber raft. He had been looking for them, he said, after giving the situation some thought.

"I live in Anchorage," the man said, "and I come fishing all the time. To tell you the truth, I think you hooked that fish first. You deserve it."

He handed the fish to the older man.

"There are not very many places that would happen," said Hanes. "He made the guy feel really good."

Steve Mahay, who has guided for more than twenty years on the Susitna and Talkeetna rivers, said he sticks with the business because he "likes seeing people laugh and smile, and making them happy."

On the other hand, not everybody on the water is happy all the time.

Once, said Mahay, he took a former Secretary of the Navy fishing and was somewhat dismayed to discover the man did not know boats. In fact, he seemed somewhat uncomfortable around them. He was a political appointee, said Mahay, not an up-through-the-ranks Navy man.

"I almost dropped him in the river," said Mahay. "He wasn't the most athletic person. I was holding his hand real hard. I could see the headlines."

Everyone made it home safely.

Mahay said he doesn't mind taking groups of foreign tourists fishing, and he has had many good experiences. But he has also had some bad experiences.

On the Susitna, many times guides simply drop fishermen in prime spots for hours of king salmon fishing in one place rather than fishing from a boat like on the Kenai River. Sometimes, though, guides get a little uneasy about what might happen on shore.

"I had a boat load of Italians who spoke no English," said Mahay. "It was a nightmare. You couldn't guess how many fishing laws they could break in an hour. It was catch-and-release, and they were planning to keep their fish."

Mahay said such groups of fishermen who demonstrate no respect for Alaska fishing laws should be charged double, just for the aggravation.

Reuben Hanke, the long-time guide for Harry Gaines Fishing, can manufacture his own aggravation with no help from others. Hanke, who is a host of the nationally known *America's Outdoor Journal* television show, said he was once filming an ad segment for the program in Togiak. He was standing in a flat swamp, surrounded by ducks, and a beaver was swimming across the river. It was a beautiful, picturesque scene, as Hanke fly-cast for trout.

"Those guys," he said of the film crew, "are real artsy. Everything's lined up. I have only three words to say and I call it 'America's Home Journal.'"

Repeatedly, Hanke botched his three words, mouthing everything but the right phrase. Things deteriorated for twenty minutes.

"Finally, I threw the rod in the river and I shouted a few obscenities," said Hanke. "They got that on tape. It was a lot easier to catch fish."

Sometimes it is easy to catch fish, even if you are not yet an expert. Take the case of a young Alaska man named Casey who was heard jokingly ridiculing the leading catch-of-the-day on Ship Creek in Anchorage because it was "only" a 45-pound king.

This story that the teller wishes to keep far removed from his name could make you nervous. The guide had a client who was a very quiet, somber fellow. The man caught a gigantic king salmon, not only a keeper, but big enough to be considered as a trophy mount.

"This," said the guide, "is a mounter."

And what did our friend say?

"Well, I'll mount it if you hold its head."

Da-dum-dum. Drum roll, please.

Once, guide Bob Saxton had some anglers out on Deep Creek on the Kenai Peninsula. Fishing was so good they stayed out a bit late and did not beat the expiration of daylight back to shore.

"We had to return to shore by flashlight," said Saxton. "We had to clean the fish in the dark, but we just shined the car headlights on them. We were fine."

"Fine" is an understatement to describe how things went for Clint Moeglein, an Alaska teenager, when he caught a 91-pound, 10-ounce king salmon in 1988 on the Kenai River. At the time it was considered the fourth largest salmon taken by a sport fisherman.

This was kind of proving the theory that world record-holder Les Anderson wasn't the only angler capable of catching king-sized fish.

When the fish hit, Moeglein was surprised. This was a powerful beast. It took off running so fast that he forgot to remove his thumb from the spool and burned the skin.

"He jumped out of the water three times," said Moeglein, giving him a good glimpse of the scope of this beauty. "I thought it was 75 pounds."

Moeglein, who along with some friends worked for Fun Fishing With Tex, brought the fish in to be weighed and measured officially, and caused a sensation. It was 58½ inches long and 36-3/8 inches around.

"I'm just shaking," he said after learning how big the king was.

As word spread about the size of the fish, people began driving by to admire it. Moeglein telephoned his parents to let them know this was a fish that had to be mounted on the wall. Their reaction?

"They had a cow," he said.

The fish seemed almost as a big as a cow.

Bob Penney's best catch might not even have been a fish. Penney is a prominent Anchorage businessman who has made a name for himself as an accomplished angler and as the founder of an organization that lobbies for sport fishermen's rights.

About ten years ago he was fishing with a man from Chicago and anxious to show off his new silver salmon fishing rod. After catching a silver of his own, Penney let the man borrow it.

Boom! The man hooks into a hard-fighting fish, and the fish pulls the rod right out of his hand. Wave bye-bye.

"That was my brand-new rod!" Penney yelled.

So Penney grabbed another fishing rod and tried to cast for the rod floating downriver. But on his first cast, he caught a fish. How inconvenient.

"I'm thinking, 'Damn, I've got to get this thing in the net quick. I want my rod back,'" said Penney.

He reeled in the fish swiftly, and as he pulled it to shore, someone shouted, "Look!" The fish had two hooks in its mouth. One was the hook from the original lost rod.

"I hooked the fish and got my rod back," said Penney. "It was like *The Sword and the River* instead of *The Sword and the Stone.*"

A big silver salmon weighs 15 pounds, much smaller than king salmon, but they can fight more fiercely. Beyond that, when it comes to fishing for silvers on the Kenai River, the angler is usually going out in colder weather.

Attendance on the river drops off in August and drops dramatically come September, when early morning temperatures can dip below freezing. The fish are still in the river, though, so if anglers overcome their fear of cold weather, they can still catch fish.

One angler who never worries about the big chill is Anchorage fisherman Chuck Tozer. He annually fishes for silvers in October or November when everyone else is home lighting the fire. Frequently, snow has fallen by his late-season excursion, but he remains undaunted. The latest date on the calendar Tozer has ever attempted to chase silvers is Thanksgiving.

"It was very cold," he said. "So cold that you delayed going out until about 11 A.M., just so you could get the daylight. It was so cold the ice froze the eyelets on the pole."

A portable heater was on board, and fishermen wore snowmobile suits for insulation.

"We caught silvers 8 to 10 pounds and even a 15-pounder," said Tozer.

At colder temperatures, of course, the river can freeze, too.

"You just go out to the main channel. That doesn't freeze," said Tozer, who admitted there are easier ways to obtain salmon.

"Go to Carr's or Safeway," he said, referring to Alaska's big-name grocery stores.

6. Catch Anything You Can

When you have been a fishing guide on the Kenai River for thirteen years, you may think you have seen everything. But no matter how long you have been out on the water, something can happen to leave you speechless.

Murray Fenton, who with sibling Mike operates Fenton Brothers Guide Service, was on the river with four people early in the morning on a rainy day. All the anglers were protected by some type of rain gear. The women were wearing clear plastic pullover hoods.

"One of the gals' rain hoods came unsnapped and flew into the river," said Fenton. "We fished all day and caught a bunch of fish. Over the course of ten hours we worked our way eight miles downstream.

"The same woman had a fish on and was fighting and fighting it. It appeared she had lost the fish, but then she reeled real hard and pulled it in—she caught her hood. We figured the fish was probably wearing it."

Another time Murray was the guide for two Colorado couples and the fateful words in their greeting were: "We've never been fishing before." As Fenton put it, "They warned me."

Almost immediately, one man had a fish on and he didn't have the slightest idea what to do. As he tried to bring the fish in, he hit Fenton in the face with his line. Fenton told everyone to put their rods up so they wouldn't get lines tangled with the fisherman. Well, they all reeled their lines in, but they were standing around the boat watching, with poles in the air. So Fenton ordered them to put the rods down in holding trays. Everyone complied, including the man with the fish.

Fenton yelled, "Not you!"

The man lost the fish.

Of course, it was a big king salmon. Aren't they all when they get away?

"I've had them so big they look like alligators," said Fenton. "Oh yeah, the biggest ones always get away."

Fenton has had fish jump into his boat, not once, but twice.

About ten years ago, he was guiding a woman from Green Bay, Wisconsin, who hooked into a salmon.

"Her line went slack and I thought we lost it," said Fenton. "She kept reeling, though, and all of a sudden, there's the fish. It just launched itself and landed flopping in the middle of the boat. It left scales from one end of the boat to the other. It broke my CB radio. We were just laughing."

That suicidal king salmon weighed 50 pounds.

The second time Fenton witnessed such an eye-widening occurrence, he was guiding on the nearby Kasilof River with three adults and a boy about ten years old in a drift boat. All of the adults had caught a fish when the youngster's turn came. He hooked into a salmon and was fighting it.

"It was kind of murky water and you couldn't see down deep," said Fenton. "I was looking out one side of the boat, getting ready to net it and I hear a splash and 'Thud.' The kid goes, 'Wow, how did that happen?'"

Most amazing, it wasn't the same fish.

"He reeled his fish in and we let the other one go," said Fenton. "That kid was confused."

Although he did not hit the trifecta, on a third occasion Fenton said he saw a salmon leap out of the water and hit a fisherwoman right in the chest, land on her lap, and then roll back into the water. Scared her to death.

Another time fishing with some senior citizens, a king salmon fight lasted three and a half hours.

"They handed it back and forth," said Fenton. "They just couldn't turn that fish. They didn't have the horsepower. We went for miles in circles."

Usually, guided fishing trips on the Kenai River end at 6 P.M., but it took until 7:30 that evening for the hooked fish to be landed.

It was worth the struggle, though, because it weighed 73 pounds.

A terrific fish, but only the little brother of the personal record 88¼-pound king salmon guide Raymond McGuire helped bring in. It was just over 60 inches long, too. The man who caught the fish in 1994 had no conception of how impressive it was.

"The guy who caught him wanted to let it go," said McGuire. "I told him that was an exceptionally large fish. We came to the conclusion that it was a big fish and he had to help me lift it out of the water."

McGuire said he once had a careless client who disregarded his advice and placed a rod between his legs, only to have the rod shoot out and drop in the river. Luckily, it got snagged on a nearby log and was rescued.

Another time McGuire caught somebody else's $300 rod. When he brought it in there was an 18-pound silver salmon attached. Now that was quite a catch.

"He'd been dragging it around," said McGuire of the fish. "You never know what to expect."

Nope. Like the time McGuire had an airplane pilot from Tennessee out fishing with him from shore on the upper Kenai River.

"I turned around to talk to someone else," said McGuire, "and when I turned back to speak to him he had disappeared. The bank gave way! He fell in over his head, but he bobbed up about ten feet away."

Murray Fenton isn't the only lucky guide to lure fish to his boat without cooperation of rod and reel. Bob Junglov of Catch-A-Lot Charters said he had a woman from out of state fishing on the Kasilof River and it was a good day, with anglers catching 40- to 50-pound king salmon.

"We hooked into one and when it was jumping for the fourth time, I said, 'This fish is going to jump into the boat.'"

Almost.

The fish jumped, but even though its effort was true, its dive was short. The fish clobbered itself by hitting its head on the side of the boat.

"It knocked itself woozy," said Junglov. "It was pretty docile after that. Denting the boat was the worst part of it."

Kasilof River guide Jeremy Baum said dealing with beginners can be interesting.

"We're floating the river and people ask, 'Which way is the river flowing?'" he said. "Duh, the way we're going. Last time I checked the river runs to the ocean."

Other beginners have been so scared they were going to be pulled into the river by a fish that they could barely fish, he said.

Sometimes fish do outsmart the smartest fishing guide.

Bill DeAvilla of Bo's Fishing Guide Service remembers the time about a decade ago when he hooked a large king salmon, but it swam into a rock pile on the Kasilof River.

"I eased the boat in and dropped my anchor," said DeAvilla. "I took my right-hand oar and measured the water. It was knee deep. And then I proceeded to step off the left-hand side of the boat and sink out of sight. And the boat took off downriver."

What a revolting development that was.

"It was a nice, sunny day," said DeAvilla, "about sixty degrees. But that water is awfully cold. I fished barefoot the rest of the day. I had my pants rolled up, socks on the floor drying out, hip boots drying out. The clients laughed and so did the boat behind me. It was on video. They lost the king salmon, but they got me back."

After that event, DeAvilla said he adopted a new motto: "I'll do anything to get a fish. Even if I have to swim for them."

And he proved it.

There are such things as reject clients, anglers who show up and just make life rotten for everyone. Most of the time they can't be screened out of the mix and fishermen must spend the day with the bad apples. Once, though, guide Joe Connors took action. A trio consisting of a woman, her husband, and her brother showed up from California and climbed into his boat on the Kasilof River. Complaining began immediately, and when the woman said, "Why the hell would anyone want to live in Alaska?" Connors decided to cut his losses. He gave them their money back.

"It's the only time I ever threw anyone out of a boat," he said.

A few minutes later the husband and brother returned without her and said they wanted to go fishing anyway. At the end of the day they gave Connors the price of her trip as a tip.

Connors, who has bare-bones cabins for clients to use the night before early-morning fishing trips, said another time a woman showed up wearing a fur coat and carped about how the cabin wasn't air-conditioned and had no screen door.

"I thought, 'This isn't going to work out,'" said Connors. "I suggested they go elsewhere to fish."

Steve Shepherd, an organizer of the huge annual Great Alaska Sportsman Show in Anchorage, said he was fishing near Alexander Creek in the early 1990s with a friend from California and they kept hooking king salmon and losing them. Finally, the friend caught a king and reeled it up to the beach.

"He took the hook out of it," said Shepherd, "and it wiggled right back in the water. He ran for it, jumped in the water, and wrassled it. He manhandled it back to shore and said, 'I wasn't going to let this one get away.'"

Shepherd said he sent a video of the match between the man and the 35-pound king salmon to *America's Funniest Home Videos*.

That man knew what he was after. Which is more than can be said for the fisherman who was out with Bob Stickles of Tri-River Charters on the Deshka River in Southcentral Alaska's Mat-Su Valley. All of the fishermen were novices, but some were more beginner than others.

"This guy's rod starts bouncing," said Stickles. "The line is just singing. And the guy goes, 'There's something wrong with this.' I was dumbfounded. I said, 'You have a fish on. Get it in.'"

The man got his fish.

One of the greatest Kenai River fishing battles of all time involved a Minnesota man and a king salmon that some thought might be a world record, the first 100-pound king caught by a sport fisherman.

It was July of 1989, and Bob Ploeger, a sixty-three-year-old visitor, was out fishing with guide Dan Bishop when he hooked into a colossal king. Of that there was no doubt. Ploeger fought the fish for thirty-seven hours, an unbelievable war played out in front of a growing group of spectators on the bank, and television cameras.

On and on the struggle went as word spread that a man had hooked a record king. He just never could conquer it. The situation was so crazy, so long-lasting, that the boat Ploeger fished from had to be refueled, McDonald's sent out food, and Coca-Cola provided cold drinks.

The worst part of the ordeal was that this was no jumping fish. Sure, it was big, but everyone wanted to know just how big. However, the fish was shy and didn't really show itself. Not during the long fight, not very clearly at the end, when the desperate attempt to land it in the drift boat failed. After the long hand-to-hand combat, the fish approached a net with a four-foot-wide mouth, but could not be netted. The hook was spit and the fish vanished.

This truly was the big one that got away. But no one could actually ever prove it was big enough to break the 97¼-pound record, either. The guide, Bishop, believed the fish was in the hundred-pound class, and when it escaped he cursed and shouted, "He's off."

Ploeger said simply, "We did the best we could."

7. They Call Him Mr. Fish

Everywhere Les Anderson goes, it's the same. I'd like you to meet Les Anderson, a friend says. Pause. He's the guy who caught The Fish.

The Fish.

The big one that didn't get away. The biggest king salmon of all time. I'd like you to meet Les Anderson, someone else says. He's the guy who caught the world-record king salmon on the Kenai River.

In Alaska, this is a big deal. Since everybody fishes, everybody would like to catch a big fish. Since everybody who fishes, fishes for king salmon, they are at least admiring and possibly jealous of a man who catches the biggest king of them all on rod and reel. Such an achievement can make you into a famous Alaskan and that is what has happened to Les Anderson.

Anderson is not a publicity seeker.

He's a low-key, grandfatherly guy, who is, in fact, a grandfather. He used to be an anonymous guy. But in the same manner that the man who is once elected governor is always called "Governor," Anderson has become identified with the catch-of-the-day. Les and his fish. The Fish.

On May 17, 1985, Anderson captured a king salmon that weighed 97 1/4 pounds. The most famous fish ever caught in Alaska made Les Anderson a well-known angler, too. There are worse things to be famous for and many times they might get you on the evening news.

It's exciting enough to hook into a king salmon of any size. A 30-pounder is a big fish and can produce a major battle. Bringing in a fish three times as large is almost unfathomable to most people. It's kind of like giving birth to quintuplets. You become an object of curiosity.

Anderson, a retired automobile dealer who lives in Soldotna, Alaska, was seventy-eight years old when he took time to reflect on how his boggling catch changed his life, on how frequently he is recognized, and how often good-natured intermediaries take the trouble to make sure everyone in his presence knows about The Fish.

"Happens all the time," said Anderson. "It's almost maddening. I can't go anyplace unless they say, 'You're the guy.' I really get tired of that. You almost hate to get known as Mr. Fish."

Almost.

On the spring morning Anderson went fishing with his brother-in-law Bud Lofstedt, he never could have imagined that by lunch he would be the talk of the state and the talk of the fishing world. In a sport like track and field, sometimes a record is preordained. A top runner is competing at the top of his game, is in peak form, and sets a long-sought-after record. Or sometimes a remarkable breakthrough is registered from an unlikely source. In that sense, Anderson's world record resembled Bob Beamon's long jump, a record set out of the blue that lasted more than twenty years.

Anderson was pursuing no record, was not particularly well-positioned with his equipment, and never dreamed his record haul would stand up for years.

Anderson and Lofstedt were fishing from a sixteen-foot boat in shallow water at about 6:30 A.M. It was quiet on the river since that is early in the season to go after king salmon returning to spawn. There was only one other boat in sight.

The monster king grabbed the hook and it set well. Lofstedt took charge of the boat's motor and steering, and when he gave it some gas to pick up speed, Anderson tumbled over his seat. He didn't lose his rod, though, and then the big fish led him on a merry chase.

"You could see its tail working all the way down the river," said Anderson.

It took an hour to bring the fish in, an impressive struggle, and Anderson was happy about his catch. But not delirious. It never crossed Anderson's mind that he was sitting with a record king in his lap. Once a fish is caught and brought in, it starts losing fluids and drying up, hence shrinking in weight. Anderson had no intention of bringing the fish to an official scale, but when he and Lofstedt hit shore and people gazed at the fish they were all over him. Get it weighed! he heard repeatedly.

So he got it weighed.

Anderson nearly fainted when he heard the measurements. The fish not only weighed 97¼ pounds, but was 37¼ inches around. The old record for a king was four pounds less. This fish was the Godzilla of kings.

The catch created a Kenai River fishing stampede. If there was one fish that big lurking in the water there must be others, right? Perhaps the mythical 100-pound king could be caught.

Over the years guides have offered rewards in the thousands of dollars to any fisherman who catches the world record fishing with them. And those same guides say that if they did catch the record it might make them rich. But it hasn't happened.

"I am surprised no one's got one over 100 pounds," said Kenai River guide Joe Hanes. "No doubt in my mind it's there. It's a very impressive record, but it's a beatable record. Every year somebody catches one within a couple of meals of the record. It will happen."

Anderson is not a self-promoter, but the mount of the fish was on display for a while at his old car dealership and now can be seen at the Soldotna Visitors Center. As lengthy as the fish is, its girth seems most impressive. And its teeth. The little razor-like chompers could be intimidating coming up at you out of the murky waters of the Kenai.

The mere sight of a huge king being brought to the boat seems to affect judgment. People always think fish are bigger than they really are. In 1996, eleven years after his catch, Anderson received a phone call from a newspaper reporter telling him a fisherman claimed he'd just caught a 100-pound king for a new record.

Was Anderson disturbed? Nope. His first comment was, "More power to him." If the record passes out of his hands during his lifetime, that's fine, he said.

"I don't mind losing it. I'd rather it be someone from Soldotna or Kenai."

Keep the fame and glory in the neighborhood, so to speak.

Of course, that big-talking, optimistic fisherman was carried away far beyond the bounds of reality. His fish was not even close to 100 pounds, not even close to Anderson's record.

The exaggeration syndrome took effect even before the fish was weighed. Getting caught up in the excitement of the catch is a far more common occurrence than actually hooking into a 90-pounder.

Tim Hiner, a veteran Kenai River salmon guide, said the biggest salmon caught with his guide service is an 86-pound king.

"That's a rarity," said Hiner. "It's more rare than you would think. We don't catch those very often. There are a lot more people who say they do than do. They don't ever weigh them on certified scales."

Hiner's educated guess from years of drifting the river is that only about one in every four thousand kings weighs as much as the mid-80s.

"People definitely exaggerate," said Hiner. "They catch a king right there in front of me and say, 'Man, Tim, he'll go 50, 55 pounds.' A lot of times it will weigh 35 or 40.

"Women aren't that way. Men are. If you have a woman on board and she catches a 59-pound salmon, then six months later if you ask her how big her fish was she'll say it was a 59-pounder. If you have a man who catches a 57-pounder and six months later you ask him how big his fish was, he'll say it was a 62-pounder. That's how they grow."

In other words, they fish, therefore they lie.

Of course, no one will be able to make a legitimate claim on any world record without documentation. The real question asked on the Kenai River each year is if there are any big hogs available at all.

"It seems to me the bigger fish are not coming in like they did," said Anderson.

No less a Kenai River fishing expert than Bob Penney agrees with Anderson's assessment. Penney, a prominent Alaska businessman, is a vocal advocate of Kenai River preservation. He frequently takes public stances for sport fishermen's rights, and he is an accomplished fisherman who has a knack for catching king salmon weighing 50 pounds or more. A part of him believes in Anderson's theory.

"If it wasn't broken by now, why should it be?" said Penney.

But a part of him also dreams of catching the big one. He is a fisherman, after all. For that reason, precisely at 6:30 A.M. on the anniversary date of Anderson's catch, Penney parks his boat where Anderson caught The Fish. Penney then pours a cup of coffee and offers a toast to the man who brought home the biggest king.

"It's in tribute," said Penney.

And naturally, if lightning were to strike the same place twice and Penney's rod bent double, he wouldn't complain. To be the man who catches the world-record king salmon is a pretty special thing in Alaska. No one will ever let you forget it.

8. Who Is That Masked Man?

At the 1996 Summer Olympics in Atlanta, basketball star Karl Malone was sitting in a room facing about five hundred reporters. He was asked if giving up his summer of fishing in Alaska to play in the Games was hard to do.

"That used to be my hideaway," said Malone, one of the greatest forwards of all time. "Until you told everybody."

Malone was joking. It is no secret that Malone's passion is fishing. He grew up in Louisiana, dreaming of checking out the Alaskan wild. When he got rich enough to do so, he bought his own home on the Kenai River. During his time off from the sport that has made him famous, the 1996-97 National Basketball Association Most Valuable Player spends as much time as possible pursuing fish in Alaska. King salmon, silvers, halibut, you name it, Malone is on the prowl.

When Alaskans heard Malone say, "I don't mind being cold or wet," they knew he was truly one of them at heart.

Gone are the days when Alaska was so far removed from civilization that planning a journey north equaled the cost, time, and effort of arranging an African safari. That means anyone who can afford a plane ticket can fly to the Arctic and the world's richest fishing grounds. It also means you never know who you're going to bump into on the water. If you think the face is familiar, there is a good chance it is.

Fishing is a pastime that cuts across class lines. Rich or poor, famous or anonymous, hunting for big fish is a kick for anyone. The only worry the facially famous have when they zoom up to Alaska is whether they can enjoy a fun, peaceful experience without being hassled for autographs.

For the most part Alaskans are live-and-let-live people. If someone's fishing on the river they leave them be. That's been Malone's experience. After a tough winter powering into the low-post and fending off other giants as he chases rebounds, the six-foot-nine, 256-pound Malone craves time to be alone.

"I love the Kenai," said Malone, who has won two Olympic gold medals in addition to leading the Utah Stars to the NBA finals in 1997. "Fishing is my relaxation. People see me on the river, but don't bother me. They just go, 'Hi, Karl.' They respect my privacy and that's important."

Sometimes celebrities fish with a certain guide only on the condition that their presence remain quiet. The late Harry Gaines said he was sworn to secrecy on many occasions, but he admitted that over the years, among his well-known fishing guests on the Kenai River were singer Kenny Rogers, actor Lloyd Bridges, and former Dallas Cowboys quarterback Danny White.

Another time word spread in Kenai that Gaines was guiding dashing actor Tom Selleck. Adoring females clamored for a meeting. If it was really Selleck, Gaines never told. Swooning fans badgered Gaines to let them know the next time Selleck came.

Numerous sports figures make the pilgrimage to Alaska to fish. Like Malone, one group of Major Leaguers bought into real estate for quiet fishing convenience.

Mark Grace, the all-star first baseman of the Chicago Cubs who played in Alaska's summer baseball league when he was in college, bought a share of a cabin near the Kenai River with Tony Gwynn of the San Diego Padres, the best hitter of his generation, and their former San Diego State baseball coach Jim Dietz, who also formerly coached in Alaska.

"I really enjoy fishing," said Grace, "but I'm probably going to have to wait until I retire to spend as much time there as I want to."

Indeed, the Major League baseball season begins with spring training in February and concludes in October. Unless those guys are really into ice fishing, or they have the misfortune to go on the disabled list with an injury, they are doomed to miss the prime fishing until their baseball days end.

Baseball players who don't face that obstacle are the boys of summer who compete in the Alaska leagues while still enrolled in college. In fact, one of the selling points recruiters use to entice top talent to the state to play ball under the midnight sun for such teams as the Anchorage Bucs, Anchorage Glacier Pilots, and Fairbanks Goldpanners is the promise of great fishing. In fact, the Peninsula Oilers are located in close proximity to the Kenai River and visiting teams pack as many fishing rods as bats for road trips there.

Surely many young men care more about working on their hitting stroke than their casting form, but for others access to the fancy fishing grounds is a major plus.

One player who made a reputation for himself in the fishing wars was Brian Loyd, a catcher for the Glacier Pilots in 1994 who was a member of the United States Olympic team in 1996, the winner of a bronze medal.

Talk about a catch-and-release strategy.

In 1994 the Pilots were blessed with two talented catchers. The manager decided he would alternate the players on a strict rotation. If you played one day, you had the next day off. That meant you could plan ahead. For Loyd, a native of Yorba Linda, California, who was an All-American at Cal-State Fullerton, that meant he would catch a game, pack up his things, and take off to go fishing well aware that lack of sleep was meaningless because he wasn't going to play the next day.

"The days I would catch," Loyd explained, "I'd go fishing all night and I wouldn't come back until noon the next day."

He drove out of Anchorage and landed on the Kenai River, Russian River, Resurrection Bay, Willow Creek, or Bird Creek. If there was a rumor of a fish sighting in the neighborhood, Loyd was there. Have fishing rod, will drive. He caught a 42-pound king salmon, red salmon, halibut, and even a sea bass off Seward. Not a bad haul for one summer.

While the number of Major League players fishing Alaskan waters is limited by their busy season, other athletes and coaches come north in their off-season, and other celebrities aren't bound by any season.

Jack Lemmon took a break from filmmaking to fish in Alaska. So did the late Raymond Burr, and Roger Moore, who once played James Bond on the screen. Singer Jimmy Buffett has fished in Alaska, as did the late Stevie Ray Vaughan. So has actor Steven Seagal and his then-wife, actress Kelly LeBrock.

Indiana University basketball coach Bob Knight has made many fly-fishing trips to Alaska. General Norman Schwarzkopf selected a remote wilderness lodge for fishing and so did Denver Broncos quarterback John Elway, who traveled with National Football League coach Mike Shanahan.

There have been rumored sightings of Clint Eastwood and Tom Cruise fishing in Alaska. Sure they came. And they caught world-record salmon, too, and threw them back. Sounds like a true story.

Every summer, professional athletes are invited to Alaska to make appearances for worthy causes. Typically, fishing trips are included in the arrangements. Seattle Seahawk football players make annual visits to a June kids clinic in Anchorage. Defensive lineman Sam Adams is a regular. A few years ago, then-Seahawk quarterback Rick Mirer made the trip and a year later his successor, John Friesz, came with tackle Howard Ballard and kicker Todd Peterson.

The Seahawks take fly-in trips to remote rivers. One year Adams, a 300-pound lineman who should be able to intimidate salmon the way he intimidates quarterbacks, had a big king salmon on his line—and lost it. It drove him crazy and he said he was going to keep coming back to Alaska until he got one.

Speaking of football types, former Miami Dolphin fullback Larry Csonka has evolved into an outdoor television sports personality, and a recent production of his is a thirteen-part series called *North to Alaska*.

In the shows, Csonka takes viewers on Alaska fishing voyages to such venues as Ketchikan and Prince of Wales Island. Csonka, a key player on the undefeated 1972 Dolphin Super Bowl championship team, utters the words Alaska tourism officials love to hear.

"You can get there," he said. "You can do it."

Hall of Fame college basketball coach Denny Crum is such a familiar sight in Alaska waters that people probably don't even do a double-take when they see him now.

Crum, the long-time mentor of the Louisville basketball club, comes to Alaska each summer to fish as part of what amounts to a worldwide tour of fishing hot spots. Fishing is what Crum uses as a distraction to forget his everyday world of recruiting young players and playing games on national television. In 1996 Crum and a dozen friends fished near Goodnews Bay and reaped a tremendous harvest of silver salmon.

"We caught silvers from sunup to sundown," said Crum, who said he took home 75 pounds of fish. "It was unbelievable. It was a great trip."

Another time Crum hooked a king salmon larger than 55 pounds on light tackle and it took an hour to land it.

"The fishing and the people are wonderful," said Crum of his Alaska visits. "It's just a great fishing experience."

Crum fishes all over, but in recent years he has participated in the annual Kenai River Classic, a July celebrity fishing tournament which raises money for river habitat protection. More than a hundred fishermen enter, and it is estimated that proceeds from a single year going to education and riverbank restoration can exceed a quarter-million dollars.

Alaska Governor Tony Knowles and Alaskan U.S. Senator Ted Stevens are among the big names who participate. In 1997, others joining them included travel writer Peter Jenkins, Apollo 12 astronaut Pete Conrad, and U.S. Senator Robert Torricelli of New Jersey.

Politicians may explore Alaskan waters as frequently as sports figures. Once, former Secretary of Defense Dick Cheney used an Army helicopter to fly from the city of Bethel in southwest Alaska to a more secluded spot on the Kanektok River.

And returning to basketball, at a luncheon kicking off the annual Great Alaska Shootout college tournament held in Anchorage each Thanksgiving, then-Kentucky coach Rick Pitino in 1996 teased the crowd with a manufactured dialogue between himself and Syracuse coach Jim Boeheim. Pitino, who now coaches the Boston Celtics, told the fans to listen and determine which school they should root for in the first round.

What's your favorite state?
Boeheim: Hawaii.
Pitino: Alaska.
What's your favorite food?
Boeheim: Steak.

Pitino: Salmon.

What's your favorite sport?

Boeheim: Golf.

Pitino: Fishing.

"We love Alaska," said Pitino.

Kentucky won the game and the tournament.

Alaska politicians should know more about fishing than most visiting pols. They are pols who know their poles. Stevens, in fact, won the Kenai River Classic once by catching a 72-pound king.

Anchorage Mayor Rick Mystrom, now in his second term, manages to break away from his civic responsibilities for regular fishing adventures. And they do become adventures. Mystrom fishes about a half dozen times a summer. Mostly he fly fishes for trout, but he makes certain to schedule at least one trip each for king salmon, silver salmon, and red salmon.

Once, about a dozen years ago, while fly-fishing for grayling at a falls near Kulik Lake outside of Dillingham, Alaska, Mystrom got into a catch-and-release competition with his brother-in-law because the fish were biting so aggressively.

One generalized popular image of fishing is that the angler sits in one spot for hours at a time waiting for action to break out. That can happen. But it doesn't always go that way. This time the activity was manic and the two men decided to see if anyone could catch thirty fish in an hour.

Cast. Catch. Release. Cast. Catch. Release. Most of the fish weighed a pound and a half or two pounds. Every minute or so there was a bite.

"I won," said Mystrom.

He caught twenty-seven fish in the time allotted. His brother-in-law caught twenty-three.

Dream fishing.

Mystrom even has a fishing tale that involves his role as mayor.

A couple of years ago, representatives of a California-based company were debating whether to locate a plant in Anchorage. The company sent a big contingent to Alaska to study the city, and the evening before their work sessions with city officials began in the mayor's office, Mystrom addressed the group at a reception.

He told them he wouldn't stay for dinner because he was going fishing right then. That's the beauty of living in Anchorage, he said. You can zip down to the Kenai River by small plane.

"I'll be on the river in an hour and a half," Mystrom said. "Tomorrow, I'll tell you how I did."

Mystrom flew the hundred and fifty miles to the Kenai, and by 9 P.M. he was on the river in a boat with his friend Bob Penney. Within half an hour, Mystrom had a strike. Penney started shouting loud enough for everyone in other boats to hear, "Get your poles in! The mayor's got a king on!"

The battle raged.

"People gave us a wide berth," said Mystrom.

It took a half hour to land the 65-pound king.

Mystrom spent the night in Soldotna and caught a 7 A.M. flight back to Anchorage. He was going to go home and change, but instead went right to the office wearing his grubby garb. He had the fish in a big garbage bag in his arms when he rode the city hall elevator to his office.

There is a kitchenette located between the mayor's office and the big conference room where the California visitors were working, and Mystrom brought the fish in there and cleaned it up a bit. Then he had a member of his staff walk into the room and announce, "The mayor just got back and he wanted to show you how he did fishing."

The aide opened the door and Mystrom—in his Levis and khaki shirt—marched into the room using both hands to hold up the heavy fish by the gills.

"I have never seen so many businesspeople diving for cameras," said Mystrom.

Everyone wanted to pose with Mystrom and the fish that, theatrically enough, was still dripping blood. Nice try on making a sale, huh? But despite Mystrom's dramatic entrance, no deal was consummated. However, Mystrom does have a great picture of himself, holding the big fish, framed on his office wall.

No celebrity who lives outside of Alaska has made quite the

commitment to the state as Karl Malone, though. For years, Malone pictured himself someday owning a home in Alaska near prime fishing grounds.

"I used to read books and think, 'I want a place in Alaska,'" said Malone. "It's just one of those great places. 'The Last Frontier.'"

Malone has averaged more than twenty-six points a game, is a perennial all-star, and was selected as one of the greatest players of the NBA's first fifty years. So he is never going to badmouth basketball, the sport that has made him a millionaire. But he does give the impression that he would fish all the time if he could.

Just in case anyone doubted Malone's devotion to fishing, in the spring of 1997 he penned a first-person story for the NBA magazine *Hoop* titled "Why I Hate Golf."

Arguably, more professional athletes use golf as a relaxing diversion than any other sport, but Malone does his best to show them the error of their ways. Malone believes that golf courses are a waste of land, and anytime he looks at one he thinks of how many bales of hay it could produce for a ranch, or how many fish ponds he could put on it.

In the story Malone makes a plea for fellow pro athletes to follow his example and go fish in Alaska.

"I think if they come to Alaska and fish with me, they would enjoy it," wrote Malone. "I catch fish, clean them, filet them, and send them back to Salt Lake. I have enough salmon and halibut to eat all winter. I'd much rather fish than play golf. I'd rather clean fish than play golf."

Karl Malone would rather clean fish than play golf? Now that's a guy who deserves a "Fishing is Life" T-shirt.

9. Whose Fish
Is It, Anyway?

There are people who might believe Jeff Lentfer is crazy. And there are people who might believe Jeff Lentfer only did what any rabid Alaskan fisherman would do.

In the summer of 1991, shortly after high school graduation, Lentfer, who stands six-foot-eight and was a high school basketball star in Anchorage of such renown that he was named the state's top player his senior year, was fishing from the bank of the Russian River with two of his former teammates.

As the anglers hauled in their red salmon, they laid out the fish in a row on shore and moved up and down the bank to keep fishing. The biggest fish was Lentfer's and he was proud of his catch. As he was walking along looking for another spot to drop a line he saw some movement out of the corner of his eye.

A bear.

The small black bear dashed out of the trees, making a run for the fish and a nutritious lunch. This is how the issue of sanity arose.

"I thought, 'Wait a minute, he's not getting my fish,'" said Lentfer.

The typical response to such a scenario is to run for a tree or another safe spot and abandon the fish to the predator. That is also the logical response, even if, as in this case, the bear may not have weighed as much as Lentfer's 220 pounds. However, there was the little matter of the bear no doubt having sharper fingernails.

Lentfer considered the situation for about a second. He thought he could save the fish. Lentfer was fast and determined.

So was the bear. They arrived at the fish simultaneously. The bear reached out a paw and grabbed Lentfer's fish. Lentfer reached out a paw and grabbed the other end of the fish. The bear growled. Lentfer snarled. The bear and Lentfer engaged in a very serious tug-of-war.

If possession is nine-tenths of the law, then surely common sense should dictate at least one tenth. Yet Lentfer refused to give in. Then things got nasty. The bear clearly had a mean streak. Unimpressed by Lentfer's commitment, the bear threw a right cross with beautiful boxing form and a claw swipe ripped open Lentfer's right eyebrow. Obviously, no amount of valor would win Lentfer the fish, right? Wrong. Lentfer fought back. He fired a punch to the bear's nose. Evander Holyfield would have been proud of the shot.

The bear surrendered. It loosened its grip on the fish and darted back into the trees. The official scoring recorded the bout as a TKO for Lentfer. The winner, though, did not leave the ring unscathed. Lentfer had to get twenty-two stitches.

Kids, don't do this at home.

This is a rare case of man out-battling bear for a fish. Was the fish worth the risk to Lentfer's health? Of course not. Was it worth the jeopardy in which it put his future college basketball career? Of course not. Will the story live on in Alaska legend? Of course it will.

Later, when he was playing college basketball at Weber State in Utah, the incident provided Lentfer with a nickname appropriate to his ferocious demeanor on the court: The Bear.

Such man-bear encounters involving fish rarely end so well for the human. In sporting vernacular it might be said that bears lead the all-time series by a wide margin. Or, put another way, sometimes you win and sometimes you lose.

Al Cratty, Jr., is a fishing guide in Old Harbor, Alaska, a community of three hundred and fifty people who live seventy miles from Kodiak on the large Southcentral Alaska island of the same name. That name is famous for its king crab—and gigantic bears. Cratty operates Al's Charters. But about twenty years ago, long before the forty-three-year-old guide got into the business, he was out fishing for silver salmon with his uncle, Carl Christiansen.

Since he grew up in Old Harbor, Cratty always knew bears were a danger to be reckoned with in that region. On that frightening and memorable day fishing with his uncle, Cratty was mauled by a grizzly bear.

Christiansen had just hauled in a beautiful, bright silver when the bear appeared out of dense bushes. The cry of "There's a bear!" went up, and Cratty tried to seize the rifle he carried with him for protection.

"Before I could get to my gun the bear had me," said Cratty.

Christiansen, though, did get his gun up swiftly.

"My uncle shot the bear while it was on top of me," said Cratty.

But not before it did some damage. The bear grabbed Cratty by the right shoulder at first and had Cratty's left arm in its mouth when shot. Two decades later there is still a large lump in Cratty's arm.

Amazingly (or at least so the agitated and bleeding Cratty thought), Christiansen's rescue was followed by his request to the boy: Get my silver.

Makes absolute sense. Why waste a perfectly good fish, just because the kid and the bear are gushing blood? Never give up the fish if you can help it.

Not every bear encounter in the Alaska wilderness ends in one-on-one wrestling. Normally, the mere sight of a bear sends fishermen scurrying. Just as frequently the bears retreat at the sight of man.

No one can ever know how many crises are averted simply because a man takes a right turn on a trail rather than a left turn, or because a bear sniffs the scent of man on the wind and decides to mosey in the opposite direction.

However, once in a while human dingbats create bear encounters for all the wrong reasons. It is said bears are unpredictable mammals, but there are several rules to follow to minimize the chances of direct, dangerous contact.

People should not taunt bears, nor tease them. They should not linger in the area of a bear kill. They should do their best to avoid coming between a mother bear and cubs. And despite examples of pitched battles to the contrary, pretty much when bears argue over the fish you strained to bring in, you should be inclined to give it up. It is, after all, a worthy cause. Like your life. There might be another fish out there on the next cast.

Still, whether through ignorance or IQ deficiency, some people aren't sharp enough to leave well enough alone, or leave bears alone.

Fishing guide Dale Benson, operator of Dale's Alaskan Guide Service, specializes in taking small groups of fishermen into remote areas of the state far removed from the road system.

"I like taking people one at a time," said Benson. "It's real peaceful."

But he'll also take out more, and on one occasion when he led a small expedition to the Goodnews River area to fish for silver salmon, Benson discovered he had a couple of people along who weren't concerned about living to their next birthdays.

The group consisted of seven anglers, and as they headed to a stream, Benson led them up the beach. Where they promptly came upon a partially eaten fish abandoned on the ground. The sight made Benson very edgy because the fish was still quivering. That told him it was likely the noise they made in their on-foot approach had just then scared a bear off its kill.

Chances were the bear was lurking nearby. Chances were the bear was still hungry. Chances were the bear was working up its gumption to reclaim its fish.

"The bear had taken off, but I was nervous," said Benson, who suggested to the fishermen that they not dilly-dally.

Most of the fishermen understood the circumstances and agreed it was best to beat feet out of the area. One elderly couple, however, didn't see it that way at all.

"They wanted pictures of bears," said Benson. "When they heard there was one there they got excited. They wanted me to chase after the bear. I told them right in the beginning, 'You leave these bears alone.' Grandma and Grandpa didn't even want to fish after seeing the bear sign."

Benson led the group downstream, dropping off anglers one by one in select spots. When everyone was positioned, Benson doubled back to check on how everyone was doing. The couple was missing.

"Grandma and Grandpa are gone," said Benson. "I think, 'Oh, no.'"

Benson surmised right away what had happened. He was sure the couple had retreated the half-mile to the beach through the brush. He was convinced they had gone back to look for the bear and he had no idea what might occur if they found it. Most likely bad things, man.

Gripping his rifle tightly, Benson searched for the couple, calling to them periodically. No answer. He was fearful he would come upon two slaughtered clients. Trying to follow them through the thicket, Benson bounded over a fallen tree and stumbled, landing on a stick. It broke and poked him in the backside. He jumped straight back up in the air. Finally, Benson heard voices.

"I come through the brush and I hear, 'Here, bear,'" said Benson.

As if the beast was a house pet.

Benson emerged onto the beach and the scene stunned him. The couple had erected a tripod with a video camera mounted on it. They were standing in the open calling to the bear and trying to coax it in from the trees by holding out a cookie!

"Because they had been feeding the bears at Yellowstone Park," said Benson. "They were looking for Yogi."

Benson went ballistic, telling the people they were nuts, that this was no cartoon bear. Finally, after a long argument, he convinced them to abandon their quest for bear pictures. When Benson reunited them with the rest of the fishermen, all the others yelled at them, too.

"The rest of the people just chewed on them for putting everyone in jeopardy," said Benson.

The twosome was lucky that's all that chewed on them.

While a bear can be encountered just about anywhere in Alaska—including downtown Anchorage, the state's biggest city with 255,000 people—clearly the odds are higher for a meeting in wild country. That's prime bear habitat.

But bears roam anywhere. Residents are advised not to tempt bears by leaving their garbage unprotected by their homes. Yet it's not unusual for homeowners to awake in the night and hear a bear in the backyard. Or to get ready for work in the morning and discover a bear on the porch.

Or, as in the case of Len and Jo Braarud of La Conner, Washington, who make regular annual fishing trips to Southeast Alaska, to have a bear stalk them on a sidewalk of sorts.

The Braaruds, who were fishing for both king and silver salmon, were accompanied by another couple at Waterfall Resort on Prince of Wales Island. They were walking by an old cannery when they met their surprise visitor.

"We were out for a nice stroll on the boardwalk after a day of fishing," said Len Braarud. "We look up and a bear is coming towards us right on the boardwalk. A typical Southeast blackie. He'd rip your head off."

The boardwalk was very narrow, certainly not wide enough for the group of humans and a bear to pass each other without slow-dancing familiarity. There was nowhere to go on either side since it was a fairly long drop.

"The bear was a hundred feet away," said Braarud. "Close enough. I was just glad I was not the lead person."

What to do?

The gang of four began singing. Loudly. And walking away, very slowly. The perplexed bear watched their performance for a little while, kept advancing towards them for a little while, then decided these noisy folks weren't worth much bother and abruptly jumped over the side of the boardwalk.

Whew. Back to fishing.

The fact is, even if a bear isn't out to get your fish for an easy meal, it might just be hanging out in the area you choose to fish in. Which still doesn't mean you should make friends with it.

Kenny Bingaman, operator of King-Sized Adventures, a Kenai River fishing guide service, is well aware bears share his Soldotna neighborhood. They also share an interest in fish. However, even the hungriest bear when sated by a protein-filled dinner of king salmon is likely to be in a very good mood.

One evening, Bingaman's nine-year-old son, Billy, was preparing the family boat to go fishing. He looked up to see a grizzly playing games.

Playing games? Really. This is what Bingaman and his son saw: a hefty bear, probably three years old, repeatedly throwing and retrieving tires normally used for dock support and preventing shore erosion.

"He was throwing them and chasing them," said Bingaman. "He did it over and over. It was unbelievable. It was unreal. He had a great side arm. I don't think I'll ever see that again."

For two and a half hours, from a safe distance, the Bingamans clicked off pictures and watched the bear fling the tires into the water, jump into the water, and haul them out.

"It was like a dog playing," said Bingaman.

Nobody was saying, "Go fetch," though.

Never has been seen such a happy-go-lucky bear. While this was a one-time event, the bear was not exactly a drifter, either. It stayed and stayed and stayed in the area—for about ten days. Every time the Bingamans ventured outdoors they had to watch out for Mr. Bear. And every time they went inside for the night, Mr. Bear ventured over to see what kind of leftovers were left at the fish camp.

"He was in my boat trying to get in the fish box," said Bingaman. "There was just the slime left in it. He lifted the fish box and looked inside. He made us pretty nervous for a couple of weeks."

It's certainly convenient when a bear sticks around long enough to pose for pictures, but most times when people come across bears they are too scared to press the shutter. And most times the bear vanishes so quickly there is no time to point, focus, and shoot.

Alaskan fisherman Greg Bill recalls the time about twenty years ago he was fishing for red salmon on the Russian River with a good friend who was a cinematographer. Their fishing was interrupted, though, by the sudden arrival of the circus.

"A moose crashes through the trees, a calf, and it's being chased by a bear," said Bill. "They jump in the river and swim across. The fishermen scattered. We couldn't get out of the way fast enough."

So to speak. They actually did get out of the way fast enough that no one was harmed.

And the cinematographer?

"He didn't have his camera with him, of course."

That was a bear with moose meat on its mind, but bears'

lust for salmon should never be underestimated. Salmon is a favorite meal for the big, hairy creatures, who sometimes go to extraordinary lengths to feed their sweet tooth.

Charley Brown of Charley Charters was fishing Alexander Creek about 1990 when he saw something happen with his own eyes that opened them quite widely. A bear used to wander around the vicinity, and fishermen and guides knew to be on the lookout.

"It showed up all the time," said Brown. "I'd seen him get out there in front of people splashing around catching fish."

However, this time the grizzly seemed determined to take possession of one particular fish. A woman fishing from the bank caught a salmon and tucked it into her backpack. The bear came shooting out of the woods on the run.

"It knocked her down and took the fish away," said Brown. "That bear had been there waiting."

Now that's a fussy, fussy, fussy bear. Good thing it wasn't Jeff Lentfer's fish. He would have wanted two out of three falls.

10. Grin and Bear It

There is one difference between the way humans fish and the way bears fish. Humans use rods and reels. Bears can just reach into a flowing stream and pluck out a fat, juicy salmon. But that's not the only popular method employed by the big fellas.

Bob Stickles of Tri-River Charters in Talkeetna likes to tell a story about a guided trip he led to Clear Creek, one of the tributaries of the Susitna River. He had a group of four guys with him from outside Alaska, and on this day the fishing was slow. They glanced up across the creek and what did they see but a big bear.

"About fifty yards away from us there's a bear who sticks his head under the water and pulls out a fish," said Stickles.

One of the fishermen looked on enviously as the bear started munching away on its catch, and said, "Why can't we do that?"

Stickles eyed the guy and responded, "Go ahead, walk on down there and stick your head in the water and pull one out."

The man did not take him up on the idea, which made Stickles happy because he stresses a very specific philosophy when it comes to sharing an area with a bear.

"If the bear wants this particular place," he said, "you go away."

This bear certainly deserved style points.

Sometimes you have to wonder if the bears are smarter than the people or the people are smarter than the bears. It's both a blessing and a hazard that the Alaska wilderness is densely populated with grizzly bears and black bears. It's also pretty densely crowded with fishermen. Both species must learn to share and share alike when it comes to the territory and the fish or else there will be casualties.

Steve Mahay, who has been guiding in the same Susitna River area as Stickles for more than twenty years, said the bears frequent the woods near the prime fishing grounds and he preaches to clients that they must be cautious. He reminds them that these bears are not in the zoo behind bars, but are wild creatures.

"These people are in a totally foreign environment," said Mahay. "There are grizzly bears. And people have been mauled. We like to play on that."

A common occurrence in the Big Su region, as the Susitna is frequently called, is the sight of fishermen who tie off their catch on a stringer underwater. The fish stay fresh in the cold river water. This is not the wisest course of action, though, especially if the fishermen leave the catch out for a long time or are silly enough to do so overnight.

"The bears will come down the row and chew the fish off the stringers," said Mahay. "Or a beaver will come along and steal them, too. People will get up in the morning and accuse the others of stealing their fish."

Big arguments follow while the bears are probably lying in the trees chuckling.

It is much better to bring along a cooler to hold the fish, or if no cooler is handy, place the fish on shore under a cache of sticks. Neither protection is guaranteed to be infallible against the on-slaught of bears who have wised up and know the drill after years of observing humans.

Once, said Mahay, an angler fishing Clear Creek was deter-mined to hang on to his fish. He thought he could outsmart bears by bringing the salmon to bed with him. So he brought fish into his tent for the night.

"His idea was, 'This bear is not going to get my fish,'" said Mahay.

That was a very optimistic outlook. Bears, though, have a superior sense of smell, and one bear's nose led him right to the tent. In the middle of the night, the bear sniffed out the fish and made its move. It pounced on the tent and knocked it down on the guy, who was yelping for help. Then the bear swung a paw much like a cat, going after the fish. The terrified man was ready to surrender not only the fish, but his wallet and checkbook. Luckily, he made so much racket Mahay and other guides figured out what was happening and came to his rescue.

"We scared it away," said Mahay. "He didn't take a fish in his tent again."

Bears do not recognize artificial human boundaries. It's not as if putting up a tent and building a fire or parking cars in a circle will cause bears to stay away. Bears are curious and they are used to getting their own way. And it's not as if any caribou or moose they meet in the wild is going to be tougher than they are. Most of the time, if a bear wants something it can get it.

Any belief that setting up camp is a protection against the invasion of grizzlies is perpetuating a false sense of security. While they rarely attack people, bears are famously unpredictable. A bear might walk through the neighborhood and never give a person a thought, or it might want to check out what to him is an unfamiliar animal.

One thing bears know for sure is that salmon in rivers and streams are there for the taking and if it so happens that a person did the work for them piling fish up in a nice, neat little stack in a cooler, or other container, they will investigate to see if they can swipe an easy meal.

During the summer of 1997 some bears discovered that fishing for fish on land could be more profitable and less work than fishing the Kenai River. They raided coolers and actually prowled for leftover fish scraps near picnic tables.

Gradually, they grew bolder and started chasing fishermen. One poor man was harassed back and forth across the river three times. The anglers made the choice to drop their fish when a bear came after them, and that unfortunately taught the bears human beings could be a source of a plentiful supply of fish.

Once a bear chewed up a hat that was abandoned by a fisherman in flight. Another time a bear went after a small boy and his dog who were entering a motor home.

Occasionally, though, a visit by a persistent bear to a camp along a fishing stream produces a confrontation ending with the death of the bear. Such an incident occurred at the Russian

River ferry campground along the Kenai River that same summer.

A pesky bear stumbled into the midst of a sleeping crowd of fishermen on a July night and turned the place inside-out. The scene seemed as wacky as a Marx Brothers movie, except the potential danger outweighed the potential laughs. One man was the first and most dramatically to be awakened by the unwelcome and untimely arrival of the brown bear. He was sleeping inside his tent when the bear climbed on top of him and started biting his leg.

The bear, which had swum across the Kenai River, ripped a hole in the tent and crawled in. The sheer bulk of the bear leaning on the man woke him up, and the circumstances naturally startled him. It would be hard to blame him if he thought he was dreaming. No such luck, though. His abrupt movements caused the bear to back off and that bought him some time. Although it might sound ludicrous, since this was no Halloween trick-or-treat situation, the man then wrapped himself in the tent.

That quick-thinking move gave him the appearance of being a larger animal and gave the bear pause. It worked. The bear started to run away.

However, the bear promptly ran into a group of tourists. The tourists retreated to the ferry dock landing and seemed trapped at the edge of the water by the very wary and agitated bear. By then everyone in the campground was awake and darting around, either frightened of the bear and running from it, or trying to find it. The activity distracted the bear and turned it away from the tourists, but it began running around the campground, pausing only to bite the tire of a motor home.

Then it chose the wrong guy to pursue. A man carrying a .44-caliber handgun was endangered, and when he couldn't scare the bear away, he fired repeatedly. The shots killed the bear, ended the threat, and brought the havoc to a close.

Not every close call with bears is as frenetic. Many encounters are shorter in duration and even unfold in a kind of casual slow motion.

Cooper Landing guide Gary Galbraith, whose homestead is in the same Russian River area, often takes clients by boat to a wooded riverbank and lets them off so they can fish from shore. One time a fisherman had a big trout on his line and was very excited. He was also wrapped up in what he was doing and not paying close attention to his immediate environment.

Galbraith noticed his client working the fish and wandered over to help him, or at least offer encouragement. While standing by the man, Galbraith heard a rustle in the trees.

"I saw a bear lying there eating a salmon," he said. "It was only twenty feet away."

Given that bears can cover twenty feet in about 1.2 seconds, there was no margin for safety. The good news was that the bear was preoccupied and sating its hunger. The fisherman was preoccupied with his own fish and loudly informed Galbraith, "I got a big one!"

Galbraith calmly replied, "It does look like a big one. It's probably the size of the fish that bear has."

The man turned around and saw the bear and reacted strongly: "Holy shit!"

Galbraith's next statement was an important instruction. "Don't run," he said.

But the bear was perfectly content with its own fish and let them retreat peacefully.

Alaskan wildlife artist Jon Van Zyle and his wife Charlotte take numerous fly-in fishing trips to remote streams and rivers in unpopulated areas across Cook Inlet from the cities of the Kenai Peninsula. The flights by small plane are very short, a half hour or hour in length, but you don't have to go very far into the trees in Alaska to escape civilization. When they travel to such places, often to chase silver salmon, the Van Zyles follow the commonly accepted advice of going heavily armed.

"We take shotguns and pistols," said Char.

They haven't had to use them for self-defense, but they find it comforting to know that in close quarters they have protection. Jon Van Zyle said that is important.

"It's so tight in the woods," he said. "They're right there in the tall grass. You know they're there. You see bear scat and you hear noise."

Once Jon Van Zyle was fishing with a group of people, including an eight-year-old boy.

"The little kid had just caught a red salmon," said Van Zyle. "He unhooked it, put it down in the grass, and went back to fishing. All of a sudden a big paw comes out of the woods. The boy sees it and starts yelling, 'Hey bear, that's my fish!'"

The kid was bold enough and loud enough. The bear got scared and ran away, and the boy got to keep his fish.

The Van Zyles fish so frequently and have been fishing Alaskan waters for so many years, however, that it was inevitable at least once they would have an up-close-and-personal visit from a bear interested in their fish.

Many years ago, about 1982, the couple was accompanied by Char's high-school-aged daughter Michelle on a fishing trip to Shell Lake, a spot near the famed Iditarod Trail. They took a little boat to a creek to fish for red salmon and had a good day.

There is a lodge located nearby and a youngster lived there who owned a dog. Jon saved the fish heads for the kid to feed to the animal. The Van Zyles were staying at a little cabin about a mile from the lodge, and when they docked the boat Jon gathered up the fish heads and decided to take the mile walk to deliver them.

Char and her daughter unloaded the equipment from the boat, which was about 100 feet from their cabin. They moved the gear in a relay, hauling it out of the boat, piling it up on the ground, and then taking it on to the cabin. After bringing the first load of stuff up to the cabin, they were about to return to the boat. Among the things still on the ground right next to the boat was a bag with the fish they caught.

"I turn around and there is the biggest black bear I've ever seen in my life," said Char. "It was in the boat. He was checking out the fish smells. Then he raised his head and he was watching us. Of course the shotgun was still in the boat—with the bear."

Char and Michelle smelled of fish and they had a puppy with them. An ideal combination for attracting the bear right to the cabin. Char quickly brought the dog into the house and locked it in. She was also packing a .44-caliber pistol, and even though she didn't want to shoot the bear and wasn't sure how much of a wallop the gun would have if she did, she thought it would be useful in scaring the bear away.

Char pulled out the gun, pointed it to the sky, and fired a shot in the air. Bang! The report was explosive and deafening.

"That bear went out of that boat and up the bank, and it was gone like that," she said, snapping her fingers. "I was totally awestruck at the speed that bear moved." Char ran to the boat, jumped in, and grabbed the shotgun. The bear did not return as they finished unloading and toting the equipment to the cabin. A little while later Jon came back. Was he racing to the rescue because he was worried by the sound of the gunshot? Not quite.

"I never heard a thing," he said.

When they flew out at the end of the trip, the Van Zyles could see three grizzly bears roaming along in flats below.

"They're not as big as our bear," said Michelle.

11. Fishing as a Spectator Sport

A river runs through it.

Well, close. A creek, Ship Creek, runs right through downtown Anchorage, creating the most extraordinary fishing opportunity in any major American city. There is nothing else like it in the nation. A city of 255,000 people with an annual king salmon run swimming through it.

Two blocks from the heart of Anchorage, king salmon weighing 50 pounds or more are available for the plucking in mid-summer. Fifteen-story buildings mark the skyline, horns beep from backed-up traffic congestion, but in the midst of the hurly-burly of big-city life is a nearly idyllic, pastoral scene. Albeit a crowded scene.

The dark green waters of Ship Creek rush past. Men and women by the hundreds line the banks fishing, or stand knee deep in hip waders seeking to bring a big fish home for dinner.

The season is short, but at the height of the run in the first half of June, the Ship Creek Salmon Derby offers cash prizes to those who catch the biggest fish. For ten days a festival-like atmosphere prevails.

Determined fishermen fish, vendors with hot dog carts set up shop, derby officials sell souvenirs, and families bring their children to the edge of the water to watch the fishermen fish and the fish fight their way over a falls.

How rare is an urban fishing contest like this?

"It's the only derby in the country in a metropolitan area," claimed Wayne Carpenter, the derby chairman.

In terms of angler hours spent pursuing fish, the fishery is one of the most active in Alaska, second only to the famed Kenai River.

The derby has a snazzy logo that is quite eye-catching. Playing up the proximity to downtown office buildings, it features a picture of a businessman wearing a suit and hip waders. The great irony is that it's not symbolic, but was inspired by a real person who in 1992 showed up to fish in this great combination attire. Instead of eating his lunch, the intrepid fisherman made a habit of going fishing.

On a sunny evening, when most people are off work, just try to find a parking space by the creek. Insanity rules—in more ways than one. It's stunning what someone will do to try to win some of the $25,000 worth of prizes simply by catching a fish.

Like cheat.

When a fisherman catches a king in Ship Creek, he rushes to the log cabin headquarters where the scales are kept, heaves his fish up on a hook, and hopes for a good reading. But the officials keep a close watch on the goings-on.

One day during the 1997 derby, a fisherman brought his fish to the scales—which are available for weighing catches between 6 A.M. and 10 P.M.—and aroused some suspicion.

"It looked a little bloated," said Carpenter, who is also a spokesman for the charitable agencies that benefit from the money raised by the sale of $5 daily and $25 weekly derby tickets. That turned out to be an understatement. Was it something the fish ate?

"It had three rocks in it the size of baseballs," said Carpenter. "The guy says, 'I don't know nothing about that.'"

Sure. The man was disqualified and Carpenter was disgusted.

"I am exasperated by that," he said. "I don't know too much about fish, but I don't think they eat rocks."

The man might have taken home as much as $2,500 in daily prize money or been in the running for a grand prize more valuable.

Standing in the water as the creek flows by can be risky. Especially if anglers move to one of the prime places where the creek flows into more turbulent Knik Arm. Indeed, those spots can be life-threatening if a fisherman is not paying attention, or the water picks up speed.

The 1997 derby was particularly eventful. A fisherman named Michael Armstrong made all the Alaska news reports by being nearly swept to his death by the strong tides. Armstrong, fifty-three at the time, hooked into a fish that was battling him. While he concentrated on reeling it in, he altered his footing, only to discover that he was not on level ground. He stepped off a shelf and fell into deeper water.

His life was saved only through the quick thinking and bold efforts of a high school sophomore named Blake Flaten, who tried to pull him to shore at first, and eventually two military men who were fishing nearby and saw Armstrong's peril.

Sergeant Matthew Plock and Sergeant Lee Archuleta, who were stationed at Anchorage's Fort Richardson, dove into the water. When Armstrong was flailing around in the water, Plock sought to calm him with the message, "We are the U.S. Army and we are here to rescue you."

Normally, such a pronouncement might be cause for alarm, but in this case they did rescue Armstrong from his plight. All three helpers were hailed as heroes and later honored officially by the city with a plaque and given expensive gifts by local merchants. Armstrong, who was hospitalized suffering from hypothermia, said without their help he would have died.

On a warm, bright evening, Ship Creek fishing during the derby is the best show in Anchorage. It takes patience to stand in one place and fish, and in most circumstances it might be said that anyone who drops by to watch someone fish is easily amused. Watching someone fish can generally be equated with watching paint dry or grass grow.

But the scene in downtown Anchorage is livelier than that. In a few-hundred-yard-long area there might be a few hundred fisherman. There is only a few feet of space between each angler, and they do their best not to invade each other's territory while angling for an advantageous spot.

A short distance away loom downtown hotels loaded with summer tourists, and the Alaska Railroad station. Parents bring youngsters to admire the sparkling water and try to spy the darting fish. And tourists out for evening exercise stroll to the water's edge. The fish scoot over a manmade falls, a drop of twenty feet or so, where the water is swift and churning. Those with sharp eyes who stand by the falls can pick out the silvery fish as they tumble downstream.

Non-fishermen congregate on the dirt bank or on the plank footbridge near the roaring falls. At this point the creek is a couple of hundred yards wide. On the far side, away from downtown, is an industrial area dotted with warehouses.

Where the creek narrows, just after the falls, anglers settle in on both sides. A train delivering tourists from a visit to Denali National Park, some 240 miles up the tracks, may pass by.

There is always the potential for injury among fishermen who get too wrapped up in what they're doing. Carpenter recounts a tale of one fisherman who slipped and fell in the water. Moments later, when his buddy reached for him to help him out of the drink, the friend was pulled head over heels into the water, too. The first fisherman had a boot stuck in a culvert and was being pulled beneath the surface.

"He damned near drowned," said Carpenter.

Alaska is known as the land of the midnight sun because of its long hours of daylight around the June 21 Summer Solstice. The sun is not out twenty-four hours a day in Anchorage, but when it is cloudless and bright, it seems as if it is light around the clock. Sunset is actually shortly before midnight and sunrise is shortly after 4 A.M. That doesn't stop fishermen from casting in the middle of the night, though.

"You can fish all night long—and they do," said Carpenter. "Come out at 3 A.M. and see. Our biggest complaint is, 'Why aren't you open all night long?'"

As ever, as is the case everywhere, the fishing is unpredictable.

An Anchorage sheet metal worker named Jim Grace looked like a sure bet for the daily prize one night when he landed a chart-topping king weighing 41.6 pounds with less than forty-five minutes to go before the scales closed. Grace was a happy guy—for about ten minutes. Joe Webster, a construction worker, hauled in a 45.4-pound fish moments later.

Sigh.

"I lucked out, I guess," said Webster, who fishes the derby after work each evening and was a regular fishing the creek for twenty-five years before he got this fortunate.

Perhaps the most surprising aspect of the fishing is that while there might be 15,000 fishermen on the creek during the derby, only 10 percent of them spring for a derby ticket.

The fishing is so enticing that some of the downtown hotels catering to tourists have taken to providing fishing poles for those interested in participating. Bob Bidwell, the derby's chief judge for five years, said some background education is necessary for those folks.

"The first thing I tell people from down south is there are no bass or catfish here," said Bidwell. "You're going to deal with an animal that's part alligator. It's going to pull you over."

Nothing like scaring the beejabbers out of the visitors, Bob.

Once a woman was yanked off her feet into the creek waters and when she told Bidwell about it he answered by saying, "You've been crowned by a king."

Another time, said Bidwell, a woman who watched a fisherman wrestle a large king salmon to shore said, "I'm not from here, but do they make a frying pan that big?"

A portly, gray-haired man with a sense of humor and an abiding love for the event, Bidwell is a dangerous man at creek side. Not only is he a key official in making the derby happen, he roams the banks bearing a video camera with one goal in mind. He wants to piece together a videotape so chock full of silly happenings that it will be shown on *America's Funniest Home Videos*.

Indeed, Bidwell has seen his share of weirdness during the Ship Creek Derby. He watched one fellow struggle simultaneously with a boot filled with water and a net filled with a king salmon. He pulled the boot off and was hopping around on one foot as he sought to bring the fish in safely.

Bidwell's wife, Sarah, who had a stroke, fishes from a wheelchair a few feet from the water and she's a whiz. She is one of those people who catches fish when no one else does. A few years ago, Sarah hooked into a king that fought back. After a few moments, though, it spit the hook and swam away. She nearly jumped out of her chair, shouting, "That's my fish!"

A few feet down the bank it was hooked again and she brought it in.

"She smells fish," said Bob Bidwell.

Fishing near Sarah is a coveted spot. She has actually said,

"Get ready," and had a hit. Others fish around her, but when Sarah casts, she's the one who gets the strike.

"Once there was a family of Koreans fishing near her," said Bob, "and they couldn't believe it. She showed them how to do it and sure enough, they caught salmon. Then they bowed to her. I like to say, 'Sarah, you've got your own little club out there.' She's got the reputation as the Ship Creek lady who knows how to catch salmon."

One hazard of fishing at Ship Creek is the oozing, sticky, quicksand-type mud that can swallow the unsuspecting angler who tromps across the wrong area. At any given moment at low tide, two or three fishermen may be stuck in the mud. Panic can easily follow if one foot is sucked deep into the yucky ground. Others stop to help if they see someone struggling. Occasionally, a boot must be abandoned in the mud. When two feet are stuck at once a fisherman is no longer distracted by fish, but praying that the tide is not due.

The Ship Creek Derby has become an Alaskan institution and as such is responsible for making appropriate souvenirs. There are pins, buttons, and T-shirts for sale commemorating each year's event and one slightly daffy inventor offers the ultimate souvenir for close-quarters fishing: a real (though defused) multicolored hand grenade, pin still attached.

This is the ultimate for making your own space.

Two men concluding a walking tour of the strip of creek featuring most of the fishermen were overheard discussing the scene. One man consulted his watch, worried the hot dog vendor and souvenir counter would shut down before he could return to the scales area.

"Got to get my hot dog and hand grenade," he said.

His companion considered the comment. "How many places in America can you say that?"

12. Women of the Water

These days, B.J. Thompson's reputation precedes her. But that wasn't always so. Not everyone who booked halibut fishing trips with Thompson Charters recognized that B.J. was a woman.

Guys can be funny about fishing. Some believe that it's only for guys. Some believe that a woman's place is in the home, skinning a fish and frying a fish. The chauvinists can be vocal about this issue. Indeed, the percentage of women who go fishing compared to men is minuscule. Even smaller is the percentage of women who guide fishermen for a living.

B.J. was named for two grandfathers named William and Joe and has been using the initials for quite some time. About ten years ago she had a charter that had all the makings of disaster.

Many halibut fishing charters depart from Homer very early in the morning. The skippers are certainly getting their boats ready by 5 A.M. and often earlier. Even if B.J. is the boss, she frequently has male deckhands. But this time a peculiar set of circumstances occurred.

Late in the evening the night before a charter with six fishermen scheduled, B.J.'s deckhand called in sick. Which made her slightly ill, too, because she had no one to help her.

"I was just sick with worry," said Thompson. Her husband assured her that everything would be fine and he told her that he'd send over reinforcements. About 3 A.M. there was a knock on the door of the boat. Standing there was her daughter, a young woman who is about five feet tall.

"She goes, 'Ta-da, I'm your new deckhand, Ma,'" said Thompson.

Very early in the morning, the crowd of fishermen arrived for the charter. And who are the clients for the day? Six macho men from Elmendorf Air Force Base in Anchorage.

"Big, humungous guys," said Thompson.

She looked at them and announced, "Hi guys, I'm B.J. and this is my deckhand."

The flyers looked at her incredulously. Thompson immediately told them that if they were uncomfortable, they didn't have to fish with her. She offered them either a refund or an attempt to try to place them on another boat. They mulled the offer for a minute and then one man stepped forward and said, "Ma'am, we wouldn't miss this for the world."

And the day produced a terrific fishing voyage.

"You talk about a big trip," said Thompson. "It all worked out. We caught all kinds of fish. A full limit of fish between 40 and 100 pounds each. I guess I got a reputation on Elmendorf from that trip because I take out a lot of the military. We had a great day, but I never will forget the expressions on their faces when they saw that B.J. was a woman."

Only a handful of women are licensed halibut fishing guides out of Homer. And that's true for women all over the state chasing other types of fish, as well. There just aren't many Alaskan women who do this kind of work.

Geri Martin, whose husband Sean guides for their North Country Charters in Homer, said he is the one who has always gone out on the water, and she has always worked on shore.

"I've always done the office part," she said.

Fishing for halibut means taking big boats out on the ocean and that requires being licensed. Many men who get their licenses obtain crucial experience on the water through the Coast Guard or by commercial fishing, she said, and those are other areas where women do not get involved in big numbers.

"They get their sea time in other ways," she said of the men. "There are a lot of gals who are deckhands. Some would like to get licensed, but they don't do it. You can definitely count them on one hand around here. We like having women as deckhands. It makes the women and children who do come out more comfortable."

So-called serious fishermen seem to doubt the seriousness

of most women who go fishing. Given the number of tourists who fish on a whim or because they are in Alaska, they are right in a sense. Many women on vacation in the state go on fishing charters simply as a favor to their husbands. But that doesn't mean all women are dilettantes.

Charlotte Van Zyle is a fisherwoman who is as serious as any fisherman and probably more of an expert than almost all men.

"I made a list of all the fish I wanted to catch in my life," said Van Zyle, who lives in Chugiak, Alaska, with her husband, Jon, a well-known artist. "One was a king salmon that weighed 50 pounds or more. It took me four years of trying. I was one of those Kenai River fishermen who have friends visiting from Ohio who catch 65-pound kings on the first afternoon."

However, many times the fishing spot of choice is the more remote waters of the Chewitt River or the Theodore River, across Cook Inlet from the population centers of the Kenai Peninsula. The Van Zyles take short plane or helicopter trips for one-day fishing trips to those areas. They get dropped off at a gravel bar with the next closest group of humans about a mile away. They fish for salmon from 8 A.M. to 4 P.M. and then return to a hotel or lodge in a town the same day.

"You have a feeling of remoteness even though you are only forty miles from Kenai," she said.

Of course, as anyone can tell you, being forty miles deep in the wilderness in Alaska can be like being left to wander in the Mojave Desert. That's why Char is always prepared. Just in case something goes wrong, the return flight doesn't come to pick them up, and they get stuck longer than expected.

"I never go anywhere without my emergency provisions," said Char.

She has a special vest with numerous pockets that she fills with all kinds of gear. Everything from water, juice, and candy bars to matches, flashlight, flares, space blankets, and pistol.

"It probably weighs twenty pounds," she said.

No wonder she gets a lot of teasing for bringing along the kitchen sink when she takes fishing trips. But she's a safety-first woman. And it's a good thing, because there finally came a time when everything was needed.

A few years ago, the Van Zyles were on one of their fishing trips to the small rivers in the woods they frequent. There were a half-dozen fishermen in the group, and Char was the only woman. This was a two-hop trip in which a float plane would ferry them part of the way into the fishing area and a small plane would fly them on another segment.

However, at the end of the day, when it was time to go home after catching king salmon, a wall of extremely dense fog rolled in. Fog too thick for flying. The planes were grounded and the anglers were stuck with the float plane. Would the delay be one hour? Two? All night? They didn't know.

They had eaten lunch and hadn't brought any food for an extended stay because they expected to be home for dinner. Time passed and darkness fell. The mosquitoes were so bad the fishermen scrambled into the float plane for protection. There were also bears in the vicinity to watch out for. The fog lingered.

After a while of being tired and cramped, someone in the group suggested they build a big fire outside the plane. The flames roared and warmed everyone. Spruce boughs were cut, a bed was made, and Char offered the use of the space blanket. People took turns resting.

"That was the first use of my equipment," she said. "We were wet and tired. It was like going to the Hilton. Everybody was really grateful for it. Then we got back on the plane."

By then it was 8 P.M. Time dragged and stomachs growled. There were coolers full of fish, but no effort was made to cook. For one thing, everyone expected to get clearance to fly out at any time. The window in the fog might be a small one and no one wanted to get caught wasting time packing up gear.

Instead of making a fish dinner, the gang divvied up all of Char's granola bars. Never did anything so ordinary taste so great. Char kept producing goodies.

"I'm vested," she boasted.

Back on the plane people started nodding off.

"There were guys snoring," said Char. "And everyone had that fishy smell. It was not so comfortable."

As time passed, she realized she had to go to the bathroom. She is not squeamish or shy, but she decided she was not going to go to the bathroom in front of the whole group. The argument was made that it was too difficult to climb out of the float plane, jump back to shore again, and keep an eye out for bears, but Van Zyle wasn't buying it.

"I decided, 'Tough, I'm going to the woods,'" she said. "It definitely is a handicap being a woman in that situation. I always take a coffee can (for close quarters), but in a plane, when you're shoulder to shoulder, I just couldn't do it."

She descended from the plane, waded through the water, and went in the woods. No bears.

The fog at last lifted sometime after 4 A.M., and the plane dropped the weary anglers off in Soldotna about 6 A.M., roughly nine hours later than scheduled. Breakfast, anyone?

Jon Van Zyle joked that no serious harm would have come to any of the middle-aged fishermen if they had been stranded longer.

"We could have lived off our fat for weeks," he said.

Char, meanwhile, learned a lesson about her provisions. She felt vindicated and smart for carrying so much stuff around with her for so many years. But in the future, she's decided, the main course will not be granola bars, as healthy as they be to eat.

"No more no-fat granola bars," she said. "Because what you're after in that situation is fat. We wanted sugar and fat."

Next time, she'll pack doughnuts.

Even if Char Van Zyle is often the only woman in a fishing group, she is hardly the only woman in Alaska who has had a weird fishing experience.

Melody Jamieson recalls a fly-in fishing trip to a lake in the Matanuska-Susitna Valley years ago with her husband and a friend. The journey was for several days, and they camped by the lake.

Soon after they arrived they realized they didn't have as much food with them as they thought. But since they were right by a lake they figured, "'Oh, no problem, we'll just catch lake trout,'" said Jamieson.

On the first day the two men went off to a different fishing spot and she stayed in camp. They set up two lines on sticks in their little lake and left them hanging in the water. Jamieson went about her business.

"I was supposed to be watching them," she said.

Truth be told, after a little while she started reading a magazine. While she was looking down at the print she sensed a jiggle in one of the lines.

"One of the lines was going out," she said. "I ran out to grab it and I ran right into the lake."

The line kept going.

"When the water was just above my waist I realized I wasn't going to get it."

The line was gone.

When the others returned she was drying her clothes by the fire. Score: Fish one, people zero.

A couple of days passed. The fishing was pretty good and they weren't going hungry. Three days after the notorious lost rod swam away with the escaped fish, the friend announced he had a fish on. He reeled and reeled and when he got it in he realized this lake trout had already been caught once. It had a fishing line in its mouth.

Guess whose line it was?

Prince William Sound in Southcentral Alaska is loaded with fish. All kinds of fish. Even whales. There is so much marine life that some charter companies don't even try to catch fish. They hire out to watch fish.

Marilyn Huddell of Homer Charters is such an operator. She shows off the whales. While some guides tell stories about whales swiping fish, she can tell stories about whales who show off.

About five years ago, Huddell had a woman from Florida on board her boat who said she wanted to see a glacier (no problem) and she wanted to see a whale. They came up on a mother humpback whale with its babies. The mother was apparently concerned for her offspring and swam up so close to the boat, it could almost be touched. That made Huddell's heart flutter. The client reacted strongly.

"I wanted to see a whale," she said, "but I didn't want to see one this close."

At times pods of whales have circled Huddell's 34½-foot boat. Huddell said they're frisky teenage whales, juvenile delinquents.

"They would get right behind the boat and the person with the camera," she said.

These whales were not only photogenic, but they were hams, showing off. At some point, though, there's such a thing as whales being too close to the customers. You want a good view, but you don't want to be capsized and have to go swimming in the ocean.

"It was pretty scary," said Huddell. "They could have turned us over. The funny thing was, they always knew who had the camera."

Another time, Huddell was looking for a great whale photo to use on the cover of her advertising brochure. Sure enough, she ran across a cooperative killer whale. Only it was in a bad mood and it took a run right at the boat. It leapt out of the water into the air right in front of the boat.

"It looked me straight in the eye," she said.

And scared her so badly she never snapped the shutter on the camera.

"I missed my Kodak moment," said Huddell. "He was too photogenic."

For her part, after a couple of decades working with the family business, B.J. Thompson said she feels completely accepted by other halibut fishing captains in the Homer area.

"The other skippers treat me as one of the guys and it makes me feel good," she said. She has lived in Homer for more than thirty years and was active as one of the few women in the region commercially fishing out of Seward dating back to the mid-1950s.

"It's tiring, hard work," she said of the all-day halibut adventures she guides. "But I never really get tired of it. The people get so excited about the fish and the scenery. Once you become a charter captain, I don't think you ever get it out of your blood."

The most frequently asked question B.J. hears is, "Do you guarantee fish?" And she has a ready answer. "Oh yes, absolutely, if you can catch them. The only thing I guarantee is a good time."

Once in a great while, B.J. comes across some prejudice when a client finds out the guide is a woman, but she thinks all-around circumstances exacerbated one man's reaction. The man from Anchorage was a regular customer of her husband Jim, but on this day he was placed with B.J., who happened to have a boat load of five women fishing.

In her typical welcoming speech to anglers—tailored to hundred-and-ten-pound women just coming along for the ride with their husbands—B.J. says that women catch the biggest fish. Well, the man turned around and looked at her and said, "I don't know about that. You just watch."

Of course, B.J.'s light-hearted prediction came true. The women, who were all nurses, went wild catching fish. Big ones, small ones. They were releasing extra halibut. And the man couldn't catch a single one worth keeping. This went on for hours and hours.

"I moved him all over the boat all day," said Thompson.

And there were a lot of places to try on the thirty-seven-foot boat. But when the day was done, the man was defeated.

When they got back to the dock, the man said, "B.J., I just love you to pieces, but I'll be damned if I fish on a boat full of women with a woman skipper again."

That was about five years ago, and the man still fishes with Thompson Charters. But each time he calls the booking agent he launches into a cross-examination. His main question?

"How many women are going to be on the boat?"

13. When the Shark Bites . . .

The Great Shark Hunt began by accident.

Sharks? In Alaska? Yep, they do exist. Forget the notion that sharks are only warm water creatures. There are many types of sharks and some of them do hang out in cold water. And one thing Alaska has in abundance is cold water.

Sharks are not a popular game fish and not a common game fish. But Alaskans do fish for sharks. Sometimes by accident, sometimes on purpose. Most of the time fishermen just want to be left alone by sharks and are happy to leave them alone. Most of the time, but not all of the time.

Alaskan angler Tom Condon remembers his shark adventure this way: Fishing with three friends in a fourteen-foot fiberglass boat in August of 1996, equipped with halibut gear, suddenly he and his buddies were after a wide-mouthed, sharp-toothed beast.

The group was fishing in Comfort Cove in Prince William Sound. The boat, he said, was "like a bathtub," which doesn't really inspire confidence for major confrontations.

According to the map the water where they were fishing was a hundred feet deep. It was a sunny day, but breezy, creating whitecaps on the water in the distance. Then the whitecaps got closer and closer, and the water got rougher and rougher. All of a sudden, leaping through the waves was an eight-foot shark. Instant excitement. One of the fishermen, named Joe, yelled, "Shark! Let's try to catch one!"

Caught up in the moment, everyone agreed that was a thrilling idea.

"We threw some herring on the line and trolled in big circles for fifteen minutes or so," said Condon.

A dorsal fin broke through the surface.

"That was eerie enough," said Condon, who was steering the vessel. "It was as big as we were."

Condon was paying attention to the task at hand when Joe shouted, "Look out!"

Not the words you want to hear on the open water.

"Coming right at us is the fin," said Condon. "It's within twelve feet and we're wondering what's going to happen. Then it went down and under the boat."

The sight of what he thought was a charge set Condon to thinking, and his next words were: "This is a bad idea."

About then one of the rods dipped. Fish on.

"Don't reel it in," said Condon.

Another fisherman thought Condon was being kind of a weenie and said he was going to try to bring the shark in.

It turned out the shark picked the line, took the herring bait right off it, and then cut through the line. Meanwhile, watching the shark and not watching where they were going, the boat full of fishermen had drifted out toward the main channel into much deeper water. When they looked at the charts again, they realized the water was about five hundred feet deep.

Still, there was too much activity to depart. They kept getting hits and the sharks kept breaking the lines. Once a shark swam within a couple of feet of the boat. When the fishermen quit for the day everyone was revved up. They decided they'd bring stronger, tougher gear to the same spot the next day and give it another shot.

"But we're in the same little junky boat," said Condon. "I'm concerned. This thing could plow right into us, and if he hit us, we'd be gone."

This time they went out with even larger bait, too—pink salmon.

Perhaps this portion of the trip would come under the heading of Be Careful What You Wish For.

"All of a sudden, Boom! Fish on," said Condon. "The shark just took the line, three-quarters of a spool, and ran three hundred feet. Ziiing! It went clear to the bottom and the line is directly below the boat."

The fishermen started the engine of the boat and moved about thirty feet.

"All of a sudden, our boat starts spinning," said Condon.

Some of Joe's enthusiasm had dwindled.

"I think we better cut the line," he said.

Five minutes passed and the fish decided to come straight up to the surface. You could practically hear that *Jaws* music playing in the background. The fishermen were located smack between two land banks. It was a quarter of a mile to land one way and a quarter of a mile the other. They had no gaffs in the boat and no gun big enough to do any damage. It occurred to the fishermen that a very big, very angry fish was headed their way.

"And," said Condon, "what are we going to do with it?"

The shark did not ram the boat, but zoomed away, breaking a steel leader as it disappeared. There was a lesson contained in that performance: that the shark was tougher than the equipment.

Another time a shark surfaced so close to the boat, it splashed them.

"There were about a half dozen moments out there that caused us to take a deep breath," said Condon. "It was incredible. They snapped the line like it was string."

Back on shore for the night, the fishermen were telling their yarn to the captain of a much bigger boat. When they informed this guy named Luke that they had been fishing for sharks in their small boat, he eyed them and blurted, "You guys are out of your minds. They've ripped the paint off my boat."

On the third day they went shark fishing with Luke, who had a forty-foot charter boat. Luke also had a gigantic hook, a mile of braided line, and an automatic winch on the back of the boat.

They went back to the same place in Prince William Sound. This time when they hooked into a shark, they were ready. It was a salmon shark weighing 450 pounds. Imagine what it would have been like trying to lift that into their little bitty boat.

"We towed it to the bank," said Condon. "And for one and a half hours, it kept twitching on the bank, even with its carotid artery cut. We were lucky we didn't have the right rigging. We would have had to throw the rod overboard if the shark hadn't cut the line."

Sharks can be vicious. Everyone knows that. They've got teeth that remind people of saws. Row upon row of sharp, pointy objects. And for every Condon and pals who think they're up to the challenge of hauling in a shark as part of the catch-of-the-day, there are probably ten fishermen who would just as soon mind their own business.

Didier Lindsey, a professional wildlife photographer, was on a trip to Kodiak Island to shoot bear pictures. Sitting in a fourteen-foot skiff in Kiluga Bay halibut fishing, Lindsey's crowd was menaced by a 16-foot shark.

"A shark came and visited us and circled us for fifteen minutes," said Lindsey.

One person in the group decided the best approach would be to harpoon the shark. You know, the best defense is a good offense. Lindsey did the math. Fourteen-foot boat, sixteen-foot shark. Who had the advantage?

"I could see myself like *The Old Man and the Sea*," said Lindsey. "We talked him out of it."

There's the accidental shark fisherman and the live-and-let-live, non-shark fisherman. But then there's the premeditated shark fisherman, who actually hires a guide and goes for the gusto.

Bob Candopoulos of Bob's Saltwater Safaris dares to go where no other shark guide dares to go. Or better put, Candopoulos operates on the assumption that enough Alaskans want to go fishing for sharks to keep him in business.

"It's a major intrigue," said Candopoulos. "It's big-game fishing. It's for someone who wants a 600- or 700-pound fish."

Candopoulos fishes for sharks about sixty miles from Seward. For years he heard people say there were no sharks in Alaskan waters. For years he heard that it wasn't worth the time to chase sharks. And for seventeen years he's been catching sharks.

"You don't have to fly halfway around the world to do it," said Candopoulos.

This is not fishing in a fourteen-foot fiberglass boat, that's for sure. Candopoulos's boat, *The Legend*, is fifty feet long. It seems sturdy enough to go to war representing a small island nation. He takes eight intrepid fishermen out at a time on twelve-hour trips. They pay three hundred dollars for the privilege. And they are definitely not using twine to catch the big suckers. You fish for sharks with 120-pound test line.

The salmon shark is probably the meanest predator in Alaska waters. No one knows how many there are and for the most part, no one bothers them as they run silent, run deep.

It takes big bait to capture big game, and the most commonly used attractant is a whole pink salmon. Such fish may weigh four pounds. That's a far cry from tying a little worm on the end of a hook.

A pink salmon is like a Big Gulp for a 500-pound shark. It will barely make it burp. But sharks have a mystique, a frightening mystique, and the idea of feeding a shark a whole fish does seem to fit. Although scientists have limited knowledge of many types of sharks, they do know those guys have a big appetite. And they may eat anything. One group of scientists studying a deceased shark sliced it open and found a license plate in its belly. It was not known if that was the main course or dessert.

Although Candopoulos is a veteran shark fisherman, he didn't begin taking clients to the murky deep waters far offshore until the mid-1990s.

"It's the ultimate," he said. The ultimate for fishing thrillseekers, that is. The sharks are so rugged that once they are hooked on heavy-duty equipment, they still must be harpooned and shot to be lifted into the boat. Candopoulos has been known to fire five shots of a .40-caliber Beretta point-blank into the head of a salmon shark as it was hoisted out of the water.

Huge salmon and even huger halibut are often referred to as "monsters" in Alaskan fishing vernacular. Sharks really are monsters. Candopoulos's clients have reeled in well over a hundred sharks. That's a lot of beef. Or rather, a lot of very tough hide.

Although fishermen can be spooked because of the reputation of sharks as fearsome killers, Candopoulos makes a habit of playing the movie *Jaws* in his video player on the return ride to Seward. He said it's been a goal of his to somehow hook up a machine to play the famous scary music from the film while his fishermen are fishing. That will surely be soothing.

On some trips perhaps six sharks will be caught. But Candopoulos said he believes in catch-and-release for sharks, too, and out of eight fishermen on board at a time, he might only take home three or four sharks.

"We usually fish four rods at a time," he said. "One day we hooked four sharks at the same time. You usually use the boat to help the angler catch the fish. But all four fish went in four directions. It was crazy.

"Using the boat you can knock an hour or hour and a half off the fight. Instead, they were standing there, toe-to-toe, for hours. The two deckhands and I were running from A to B to C. It took about three hours to get them all in. We landed all four, and they were all 400 pounds. One was 650 pounds."

That time the sharks came out the losers.

14. Wherever There's Water, There's Fish . . . and Wild and Crazy Fishermen

Dennis Corrington has lived in Alaska since 1967. He is what is known in business circles as an entrepreneur. And he is what is known in public-speaking circles as a "storyteller."

Which makes him a natural to talk about fishing. His stories at least have the ring of truth about them, and that's all that matters.

Originally from Missouri, Corrington has lived and fished in Skagway in Southeast Alaska and in Nome on the western Arctic coast. He used to haul crab pots and shrimp pots to Prince William Sound as well.

Pretty much everywhere he's been in Alaska, there's water. That's because pretty much anywhere anyone goes in Alaska, there's water. Lakes, rivers, or the ocean. Especially an ocean. In fact, Alaska has 33,904 miles of coastline, more than all of the other forty-nine states combined. It also has about three million lakes. There is no recent government census of bathtubs, but even without that update clearly there are lots of bodies of water where fish might be lurking.

Over the years, Corrington has gotten to know a lot of fish up close and personal. But just as you always remember your first date and your first kiss, you always remember your first Alaska fish.

Thirty years ago, Corrington discovered an abandoned miner's cabin on the outskirts of Nome and decided to adopt it. It was a structure badly in need of repairs, and that's how Corrington spent his weekends, hammering and sawing, trying to improve upon the basic amenities.

One day he was working on the roof, nailing down tarpaper,

when he heard a splashing sound. A very shallow creek ran right past the cabin, but it wasn't deep enough to drown a squirrel. By strict definition, it might have been a puddle except for the fact that the water actually moved.

The first animal to come to mind that could be playing in the water, though, was not a squirrel, but a bear. Corrington felt compelled to investigate. So he climbed off the roof, and taking a closer look at this tiny creek he was amazed to see salmon slithering past.

"It was so shallow their bodies were swimming 70 percent out of the water," said Corrington.

Thinking ahead to dinner, Corrington took immediate action.

"I smacked one of those fish with my hammer," he said.

He promptly took the fish inside the cabin and cooked it. Had a delicious meal.

Later, when someone stopped by this humble abode and asked where he caught the fish for the great dinner he was boasting about, Corrington led him out of the cabin and over to the water. The man couldn't believe it.

"That's not a creek," he said, "that's a drainage ditch."

Finding the scene difficult to comprehend, the man peppered Corrington with questions. He wanted to know what type of fishing gear he had, what kind of lure he used.

"A double-fork hammer," Corrington replied. "I brought it from Missouri."

The man said he had never heard of that kind of lure and went away scratching his head.

"He never really got it," said Corrington. "That was the first fish I caught in Alaska."

Those were the old days. Now, Corrington lives in Skagway, the one-time jumping-off point for the Klondike Gold Rush. Recently, Corrington was working on remodeling a hotel for tourists and announced to the world that he'd discovered gold on the site. Got a lot of free publicity out of that one. Enough to make you wonder if his fishing tales aren't tall tales. But, it is fishing.

Corrington's current fishing journeys are pretty much confined to Southeast Alaska. Sometimes he travels inland, toward

Canada (he innocently mentions that once in a while he forgets a map, gets confused, and just possibly strays into the Yukon Territory) and in one spot that will remain secret, about three years ago, he had a dream fishing day in pursuit of salmon.

Between eight in the morning and one in the afternoon, Corrington, his then-thirteen-year-old son, and a friend had twenty-four strikes and landed seventeen king salmon. Minimum keepers in that area are 42 inches, and Corrington swears on a stack of Jack London books that most of them were barely a quarter-inch to a half-inch too short.

"It really broke my heart to drop them back," he said of this catch-and-release test of will.

Soon after this experience, Corrington said he bumped into a man of the scientific persuasion who informed him that it takes the typical angler an average of eighteen hours of fishing to catch a king salmon in that part of the world.

As the grin spread across his face, Corrington related the story of the twenty-four strikes. The man stared at him and said, "I don't even want to talk to you." Then he uttered an unprintable word.

The prime fishing season in the Skagway area, like most of the rest of Alaska, is May to September, but by comparison to Southcentral and Interior Alaska, the southernmost region of the state experiences milder winters. Most bodies of water don't even freeze and especially not port waters of the Inside Passage, where cruise ships cruise in the summer. It may be cold, it may be windy, and it may be uncomfortable, but technically, that means it is possible to fish just about year-round.

"There was one old guy who used to live in town—he retired and moved away—and it was his claim to fame that he caught salmon every month of the year," said Corrington. "It was a little nippy. And I think he took a little nippy with him when he went out, too."

Meanwhile, back to Corrington's map-reading skills. If you look at the map you realize that Skagway is positioned much closer to Canada than it is even to Juneau, Alaska's state capital. Innocent mistakes are bound to be made by intrepid anglers who a-fishing-they-will-go.

"Once it turned out I was fishing about sixty miles into the

Yukon," said Corrington. "Duh. I didn't know. I didn't know I crossed the border."

Well, Southeast Alaska does constitute a narrow strip of land, that's for sure. There is plenty of fishing in that portion of the state. After all, it's all islands and coastline. Remember, where there is water, there are probably fish.

Actually, fish may not be the only species in the neighborhood, either.

Len Braarud, who lives near Seattle, Washington, and makes annual trips up the coast to the happy fishing grounds of Southeast Alaska, was once fishing for king salmon at Elfin Cove on Chichagof Island.

"I have never seen so much sea and wildlife," he said. "Bears, seals, eagles, whales, porpoises, all from the boat. Krill so loud you could hardly speak. It was like being in a Disney movie. And when I caught the biggest king I have ever caught, a 52-pounder, a whale sounded ten feet from the boat."

For Ken Marsh, a lifelong Alaskan who was the longtime outdoors editor of *Alaska* magazine, Southeast waters have long been a playground.

Once, said Marsh, he was on a fishing trip to Petersburg with Tony Route, another well-known writer who specializes in prose about fishing. The twosome was stationed in a cabin near a little bay where the tide would rush out to the ocean through a narrow bottleneck. Marsh was taking a break in the cabin when Route came running in with a tale.

"We were fishing for cutthroat trout, about eight to ten inches long, on fly rods," said Marsh. "Tony was standing in the water in his waders and hooked a fish. As he was reeling it in, all of a sudden a small shark grabs it right off the line."

When he realized what he had seen, Route got out of the water pronto.

"He said it was real creepy," said a skeptical Marsh, who naturally teased Route about the *Jaws* movie.

However, they were staying in a U.S. Forest Service cabin that had a logbook, and when they began leafing through the pages, they came across an entry someone had written about the sharks in the area. Made believers out of them.

More often, fishermen venture into ocean waters for king

salmon and halibut along the coast. Anyone who has cruised across the Gulf of Alaska in a sailboat or other small vessel can attest to the fact that the water can churn mightily in this part of the country.

As much as he loves fishing, Marsh hates nasty seas. He is one veteran angler who admits to having a tender stomach. However, when it comes to fishing, it is no contest—he is committed to overcoming such obstacles. Like the time Marsh was fishing off-shore near Ketchikan. The weather was really bad. It was go-home-curl-up-by-the-fire-and-drink-hot-chocolate weather.

"It was drizzly and windy, Southeast at its best," said Marsh. "It was so rough and choppy we were on our knees. We tried to stand, but it was pitching us all over. It was the swells and the smell of the diesel making me really queasy."

So why not go in if the conditions are so miserable? Are you kidding? The fishing was great.

"We caught lots of fish on our knees," said Marsh. "It's all in the arms and shoulders. We caught lots of fish and I didn't puke. So it was a good day."

Spoken like a true-blue fisherman.

15. Fishermen Do Strange Things Under the Midnight Sun

Captain Ron is used to the double takes. He is also used to people not even noticing the rare and unusual. After years of cataloguing in his individual poll, Captain Ron can say with some certainty that only one in twenty people is genuinely observant.

You decide.

When Ron Johnson, who operates Captain Ron's Alaska Adventures in Whittier, Alaska, attends fishing shows or puts up displays of the catch of the day garnered on his fishing charters, like many other captains he shows off blown-up pictures of anglers and their biggest fish. Such pictures are common. Fred Fisherman catches a 200-pound halibut and there's Fred, standing on the dock, next to the big white flatfish hanging on a hook and bearing a tag with a hand-written "200" on its belly. The anglers get souvenirs and the guides get to boast about the big catch. The pictures pretty much all look alike.

There might be seven or eight such pictures as part of Captain Ron's splashy display. With one slight difference. Tucked in the middle of the display, there is usually a picture of a fisherman hanging upside down from a hook, with a number signifying his weight stuck on his belly.

Hello?

As Johnson said, perhaps 5 percent of passersby notice the juxtaposition of man and fish. But that 5 percent demand an explanation. Captain Ron provides it. Sort of.

"The angler put up a big fight," he said. "It took the fish two hours to bring him in."

At that point, Johnson either has the questioner laughing or ready to bolt for the telephone to call in help so Captain Ron can be committed for ten days of observation.

Captain Ron has one picture of a seventeen-year-old hanging upside down in this predicament. The young man weighed 145 pounds, the fish he caught weighed 157 pounds. Captain Ron has another picture of a 205-pound man hanging on a hook. That man caught a 260-pound fish.

Do you detect a pattern yet?

"I figure if you catch a fish that's bigger than you, you should be the one to hang upside down," said Johnson. "We had to do something different."

This is not a universally accepted practice in the guide industry. Nor is it a universally accepted way to cap off a fishing trip in the fisherman industry. In other words, not everyone wants to do it. But those with a sense of humor comply after Captain Ron's urging.

The man who caught the 260-pound fish on Labor Day 1996 was one of those who had to be talked into allowing the blood to rush to his head.

"He was a little worried," said Captain Ron. "But he went for it. He labored on Labor Day."

Perhaps the most amazing aspect of Captain Ron's little joke is how few people even notice that something is amiss as they cruise by his booth at sportsman shows or fairs. Maybe because it is so unexpected. Maybe because they have been glancing at so many displays, they are bleary-eyed.

"It doesn't really register," said Johnson.

To them, it's just another man-out-of-water trick.

Chuck Landers, a fisherman from Chugiak, Alaska, remembers one incident that cleared four men out of the water faster than a speeding bullet. Or perhaps that's not the proper phrasing, given what occurred.

Years ago, Landers and three friends were fishing for king salmon near their cabin at the mouth of the Deshka River in Southcentral Alaska. They were using a large boat, an airboat with a partial covering. So only two men could fish at a time.

On this particular day, two of the friends, Bill and Bob (not their real names) had lines dropped in the water, Chuck (his real name) was watching, and Carl (not his real name) was resting in the captain's seat.

The fishing had been pretty good, and sure enough it didn't take long before more were on the line. Bill hooked into a fish and it seemed like a pretty good-sized one. Bob hooked into a fish at nearly the same time. The fight was on. Men were reeling, fish were struggling.

Bill seemed on the verge of landing his king when Carl announced, "I don't want any more fish in the boat. It's too slimy."

Sounds like a joke, right? At this point in the telling, however, Landers insisted, "This is the truth."

Well, the fish got a second wind, and it was jumping back and forth, and Bill just couldn't get it over the side of the boat. Everyone was cheering him on and was preoccupied watching him. Almost everyone.

Carl reached down and produced a .44-caliber handgun. Before anyone could object, he took aim and announced, "I'll kill it." Then he fired.

Carl missed the fish. But the bullet hit the line, severing the connection between rod, reel, fish, and fisherman.

"What are the odds of hitting the line?" said Landers. "Bill just sat there and looked at Carl."

Everyone went into shock. Not the least of reasons being that attempted assassination of a king salmon with a loaded pistol is highly illegal. Upon the telling of that tale, listeners invariably end up open-mouthed, but, Landers said, "The truth is stranger than fiction."

Within what seemed like seconds, all gear was packed, the boat was docked at the nearby shore, and the men had fled from the river.

By now the statute of limitations probably has been exhausted and no one will be arrested. But in a lifetime of fishing, that was a once-in-a-lifetime incident for Landers.

Handguns are not the only weapons available to fishermen. For less than ten dollars, you can buy your favorite fisherman the best Christmas present he ever got—a specially designed hand grenade. Just pull the pin, toss it in the water, and *voila!* Boom! Fish galore. Well, not really. (We think.)

The hand grenades for sale come in lovely combined shades of yellow and orange with green handles decorated with fish eyes on either side. Oh yes, there is a king-sized treble hook dangling from the bottom. Quite sharp, too.

Naturally enough, the company that makes these fishing aids is called "Combat Fishing" and is located in Eagle River, Alaska. The hand grenades come in a wooden box with a distinctive emblem. Creator J. Elliot Skala has emblazoned the box, as well as an accompanying instruction handbook, with a memorable picture. The design features a picture of a frowning fish wearing an army helmet with a star on it placed inside a circle. The fish has a hand grenade on its right and an assault weapon on its left. The company motto is, "If we can't catch 'em, they're not in the water."

The instruction booklet is written tongue-in-cheek and features a strong opening paragraph: "Congratulations! You've just purchased the most effective fishing lure ever developed. We here at Combat Fishing Company have dedicated our lives to creating the ultimate fishing lure, testing millions of combinations of shape, color, action, and laser-sharp hooks to bring you what our satisfied customers call 'the ultimate lure with explosive results!'"

Somehow, it is not surprising to read on and discover that this item promises "dynamite fishing."

Alaskan artist Jon Van Zyle's passion for fishing runs nearly as deep as his passion for painting.

Once, while fishing in solitude on the Theodore River, Van Zyle and his wife, Char, were interrupted by the surprise arrival of a helicopter.

"You don't expect to see something like that, but we looked up and there was a helicopter with a film crew hanging out shooting pictures," said Van Zyle. "Finally, they landed, and they had an actor with them. They were shooting a commercial. They saw the fish and asked if they could fish with us. We said okay."

Van Zyle can't remember the actor's name or the product he was trying to sell, but he does remember that the man needed lots of help fishing.

"Right away the guy tangled the lines," said Van Zyle. "It created a real bird's nest of a mess. Then, on the first cast, he catches a king salmon. He's screaming and not knowing what to do."

The gear was so fouled up that the Van Zyles had to splice a fresh line into the tangle so the man could reel.

"We gave him the other rod," said Van Zyle. "He fights this fish and he brings it in. Some guy from New York or Hollywood, and he's the happiest guy in the world. He's exhausted. There are three people helping with two rods and three lines and he goes, 'Should we keep it?'"

Van Zyle bit his tongue and then said, "I think you should keep it."

If the man had thrown the fish back after all that, Van Zyle probably would have strangled him with the tangled lines.

Van Zyle is not a stick-to-one-place fisherman. He roams all over Alaska, sometimes traveling by car, sometimes flying in to a fishing spot, sometimes traveling by boat. He can tell a story about how tough the Alaskan wilderness can be on fishermen when they're not even fishing.

Once Van Zyle and his twin brother, Daniel, also an artist, and friend Alan Lemaster, a Gakona businessman, were fishing the Gulkana River by raft. The Gulkana can be a roaring river. Or in hot, dry times the water level can drop.

This was one of those occasions, so that meant the men had to portage at various times. They lifted the raft out of the water and became porters, toting it through the brush or narrow spaces between trees.

"We were carrying it sideways to get through the willows and we come around a corner and there's a cow moose with a brand-new calf," said Van Zyle. "The calf saw us and jumped into the river."

The men stopped and stared. The big moose stopped and stared. The moose easily might have charged and stomped them.

"We never moved," said Van Zyle.

The moose started running, but not directly at them. It went after the baby, diving in the river close by. Still, it ran so near that it hit the raft as it passed.

"Momma goes after the calf, thank God," said Van Zyle. "It

took that calf five minutes to get away from us in the water. We got out of that area real quick. It was very close."

Past experience has taught Van Zyle that it's important to pack everything you might possibly need when going off to the wild. He doesn't mind traveling in style, either, so he isn't fanatical about packing light. But sometimes hard lessons are learned through discomfort.

Once, years ago on a ten-day float fishing trip down the Kobuk River in Northwest Alaska, he was chasing sheefish with his wife, Char, and another couple. This time Van Zyle found out how woefully ill-prepared he was.

Just before the trip began, the woman in the other couple informed the Van Zyles that she had some whiskey with her and that they might want to bring some along. They declined.

"None for us," said Van Zyle. "She said, 'Don't come begging to me.'"

The anglers traveled by raft, paddling and fishing, paddling and fishing. Long days of fishing followed by camping by night.

Of course, this being Alaska, it was cold and damp much of the time. The longer they stayed out, the colder and damper it got. And what medicinal remedy is handy to warm them? The liquor, of course.

"I'm literally on my knees begging for a drink of the booze," said Van Zyle.

And the woman wouldn't share.

There are provisions and there are provisions. And sometimes the little things make a difference.

When the Van Zyles entertain out-of-town guests, they are apt to take them fishing, too. About five years ago, Char's cousin Faye came to visit from California. The red salmon were in, so the Van Zyles hauled Faye and her husband, Dewey, down to the Russian River with Char promising the novices that she'd help them fish.

After some basic instruction, Faye stood on the bank, cast her line into the emerald green waters, and sure enough, hooked a fish.

"She reels it in and gets it up to the bank," said Char. "But right there it gets stuck on a log. The line is wrapped around the log underwater."

The fish was clearly not going to be reeled in without extra difficulty. Char surveyed the situation and jokingly announced, "One of us is going to have to take our clothes off and get that fish."

Dewey, the other beginner from California, proclaimed, "I'll do it." Instantly, before the others could react, he stripped to his underwear, waded into the water, and wrestled the fish to shore. The water temperature was in the forties, not exactly soothing.

Anglers on shore and in passing boats watched the drama, and when Dewey brought the seven-pound salmon in and presented it to his wife, they applauded.

"If you fish on the Kenai, it's never private," said Char.

Dewey basked in the applause, but only for a moment.

He was shivering and blue.

"It was the height of chivalry," said Char.

Chivalry may be a good reason, but chasing anything in the water means it must be dear to your heart.

Our old buddy Captain Ron remembers the time when he was out fishing and it was so windy that he anchored his boat in a bay to ride it out.

"It was howling," said Captain Ron. "Fifty, sixty knots. And a deckhand's cap blew overboard."

Sayonara cap, right? Nope. This man wanted his cap in the worst way. So he unloaded an inflatable raft and began pursuit of the hat. He rowed about three hundred yards to the beach and, astonishingly, retrieved the cap. He put the hat on and started to shove off.

Captain Ron and his fishermen on the boat watched this action from a good distance and were horrified to see a black bear jump out of the trees and begin closing the gap on the deckhand. The man had his back to the trees and was oblivious.

The deckhand casually rowed back to the boat and was surprised when everyone hurriedly raised him up and told him about the bear after his hide.

"We joked that he was our bait," said Captain Ron.

But the man did get his hat.

Fishing out of Whittier, the small town in Southcentral Alaska not far from Anchorage, means Captain Ron heads out to water deeper than any of the popular fishing rivers and lakes that dot the state.

Once, cruising around in his forty-five-foot boat, Captain Ron had some Texans aboard who were quite taken by the natural beauty of the surroundings. They were very impressed when they saw killer whales on the horizon. Then the fishermen hooked a fish and were even happier.

"Only pretty soon the line started spooling out," said Captain Ron. "And snap, it was gone."

A whale ate the fish.

Sometimes foreigners (Texans not included) provide different perspective on the goings-on. Once Captain Ron guided a group of Germans for a week, and none spoke English. He had only German-English dictionaries for assistance.

By the time they were finished, though, they had fish and he was nearly fluent in the language. Well, that's an exaggeration, just another fish story, really.

"But I did learn a lot," he said.

There was no language barrier when he had an Englishman aboard.

"It was bloody this and bloody that," said Captain Ron. "Well, he caught a bloody fish."

Likely, his clothes were never clean again.

16. Fairbanks Fishermen Can Have Fun, Too

Mike Kramer likes to say that the Gulkana River is Fairbanks's home river.

He's got a point, even though the river is about 230 miles from the Golden Heart City. It's not as famous as the Kenai River and the king salmon aren't as large. But it's a long, long way to the ocean from land-locked Fairbanks, so you've got to start somewhere.

Poor Fairbanks anglers. Avid fishermen who live in Alaska's second-largest city just have to work at their passion harder than most Alaskans.

Kramer, a one-time high school distance running star from Fairbanks, went to college, came home, and decided that becoming a fishing guide was the way to go. But there's no guiding on the Chena River, which bisects Fairbanks, so where did he pick to hang out? The Gulkana.

The vast majority of his summer clients are Fairbanks or North Pole residents. Not *the* North pole, but the suburb of Fairbanks.

The Gulkana has been a good friend to Kramer. Most of the time. There was the occasion about five years ago when he and other guides were out in a boat at the start of the season doing what he calls "scout fishing."

The water was low in late May, and mainly the guides were trying to determine if there were any fish around so they could start taking out clients. They caught the first two king salmon on the river that year and were a happy bunch.

"We were standing up, high-fiving," said Kramer, "and it was getting a little late in the evening."

115

Which meant that the light was getting a little dim, too. Well, so much for all the excuses.

"I was piloting the boat and smacked it into a big boulder," said Kramer. "We went over the top. We got airborne over it. It was a smooth rock and it kind of acted like a ramp."

It could have been worse. It might have been a head-on collision dumping them all in the river. They were all guilty of inattention, but the responsibility fell on Kramer since he was steering. That's why the location is now dubbed "Mike's Rock."

While the biggest king salmon in the world return to the Kenai River, the kings that spawn in this area and swim up the Gulkana are smaller. A good-sized king caught on the Gulkana will be a 25-pound fish. That's still a large fish and certainly big enough to create the usual fishing catastrophes and oddities that afflict fishermen.

Like the time a fishing rod snapped in an angler's hands, but the fish didn't get away.

"You're fighting the fish with the butt section of the rod," said Kramer.

Once, Kramer had four fishermen with lines in the water get simultaneous king strikes. Four on at once, and they brought them home.

"It's a real team effort to get the fish then," he said.

The most uncomfortable scenario is when a salmon takes the lure of a fisherman who is on the outside of the four in a row fishing and then runs right across the other lines.

"We've gotten the fish in," said Kramer. "Once I had a fish take two lures. It was moving upstream with the first hook when it took the second one. You think you have a double catch."

Having two fish on among four fishermen is a rarity, and four on is a once-in-a-decade occurrence, but three hookups at once is about an annual event.

"Kings are unpredictable," said Kramer. "You're negotiating the rocks. One fish is going upstream, one going downstream, one fighting. You're handing rods under arms and across the boat. Frantic would be a good way to describe it."

A traffic jam and Kramer as the traffic cop.

The king salmon may be smaller on the Gulkana than on the Kenai, but they are probably more aggressive. The greatest fishing day of Kramer's life, in the mid-1990s, stands as evidence to that theory.

All other fishing guides had cleared off the river because they thought the king run was over. Kramer had one gentleman who wanted to give the fishing a try, though.

"He was committed," said Kramer. "He was going to catch one."

Surprise. Overnight, another run of fish entered the river, so when Kramer went out, it was like stepping up to a buffet table with no competition.

"In four hours he landed twenty-three kings," said Kramer. "It was unbelievable. We had just one line in the water, and it became a game to see how many we could get. I'd say the longest we spent was forty-five seconds between catching them."

Meaning forty-five seconds of actual fishing since you can't catch a fish without a line under the surface, and it took some time for the man to release the fish he hauled in. The angler kept just one fish and released the others, but they took pictures.

Initially, they fished with bait, but after a while they didn't even bother. That didn't matter, either. The fish kept coming. The only reason they finally stopped was because the angler, a big man, was too tired.

"He cried uncle," said Kramer. "And wanted to go in because his arms were so sore."

A year later, Kramer had two men out when the fishing was nearly as good. They were catching fish after fish, releasing most, and had reeled in about ten when one man's rod doubled in half. The big one!

"He went to set the hook," said Kramer, "and the fish's head was above water. The hook flew out of its mouth and the lure just imbedded itself in his arm. I had to do a little stream-side surgery."

A fishing guide must be versatile when he's out on the river and be prepared for just about any eventuality.

Once, while fishing from the bank, a client reeled in a big salmon.

"I gave it the *coup de grace* with a conker," said Kramer, "but the fish flopped out of the guy's arms while he was posing for a picture, and went back into the river."

The fish came back to life!

"I knew the fish was seriously stunned and it might not swim very far," said Kramer. "The fisherman dove in trying to catch it and dunked an expensive camera. I knew I had to redeem myself so I jumped into the boat and started chasing it. I left the clients on the beach and said, 'I'll be right back.' I might not have come back to get them if I didn't catch it."

A Mountie always gets his fish.

"I caught up to it within a half-mile and netted it," said Kramer of the resilient salmon. "It was a 40-pound king."

Of course, it's not always convenient to jump in the car and drive four or five hours every time you want to go fishing, so not every Fairbanksan's fishing involves the Gulkana River.

Bruce Bell, who describes himself as a sporadic fisherman, makes an annual summer pilgrimage to Quartz Lake for land-locked salmon and trout, but admits there are no big-time fish to be caught there. It does, however, sate the thirst.

Better than ice-fishing, at least, said Bell, who is a former college basketball player.

"I tried ice-fishing once," he said. "That's a whole lot of standing around and getting cold. That's why I picked an indoor sport."

Once, said Bell, he tempted cold-weather fate. Fishing at Harding Lake, a popular fishery about forty-five miles south of Fairbanks, he was in a canoe when the ice shifted to his side of the lake. The canoe was trapped in the ice. He and friends panicked and tipped the canoe over. For a moment they were convinced they were going to drown.

And then Bell, who is six-foot-seven, realized he could stand up. They were in about six inches of water.

"It was so shallow that on your knees you were about at water level," he said. "Maybe the canoe tipped . . . because we were actually touching bottom."

Bell wonders if his fishing interest wasn't stunted at age four-teen, when he got in trouble fishing the Salcha River.

"I snagged some fish," he admitted.

And state fish and game department agents were on the spot to nab him for wrongdoing. Bell was already six-foot-one and the authorities didn't believe he was a youngster. They gave him such a hard time that he never went back.

"I haven't fished in that river since," said Bell. "It's been twenty years now."

Jim Whitaker, a Fairbanks businessman, enjoys fishing for pike. To catch them, he travels to the Minto Flats in Alaska's Interior, an area he calls "three hundred miles from anyplace."

From Whitaker's description, it seems most sane fishermen might want to stay three hundred miles away from pike, given their aggressive natures. But using the words "fishermen" and "sane" in the same sentence is like using "military" and "intelligence" together.

The area where Whitaker indulges his vice is crisscrossed with lakes and rivers, clear water dotted with logs and reeds that harbor a multitude of what might be the nastiest fish in Alaska waters.

"They're like catching a mad dog," said Whitaker of pike. "Until you kill them, they will attack you. They look like a barracuda, with a long snout and a mouth full of teeth. After you catch one, you keep your hands away from the fish's mouth because they are mean. Truly vicious. Their eyes are right on your hand."

Most pike Whitaker catches are perhaps 30 inches long and generally weigh 10 to 15 pounds, though the biggest pike he has landed weighed 25 pounds. When he caught the 25-pounder, it took twenty-five minutes to land.

"I played him a little bit," said Whitaker. "There was lots of open water. They run for cover."

Up close pike do not look benign.

"The teeth can cut the line," said Whitaker. "Their teeth just stick in your fingers. They're like pit bulls. They taste good once you get them, but they're hard to filet. Salmon give up. Pike fight you all the way."

Pike never had such a press agent to build up their fearsome reputation. In fact, when Whitaker starts talking about what makes the best bait for pike, no one quite knows if he's serious or not.

"I've heard of people using little baby ducks," said Whitaker. "They'll eat anything." Then he paused. "I would never do anything like that."

However, just to prove how voracious these fish are,

Whitaker mentions that fake mice are sold in bait shops as enticements for pike.

"They'll go for that," he said.

Whitaker's favorite and most dramatic pike story is second-hand, but one in which he has absolute faith. It involves his wife, Jinx, who years ago was fishing with another man. They caught a pike, brought it in, and as they were subduing it the fish took a snap at the guy. While he was quick enough to elude the bite, the reflex pull-back got him entangled with another hook that embedded itself in his thumb.

Finally, the fish was killed and the hook removed. Jinx started to gut the fish, but she felt something moving. When she reached in to pull the fish guts out, something squirmed. A mouse the pike had swallowed was still alive. When she sliced the fish open, the mouse bounded off into the underbrush. The shock had her screaming long and hard. She just stood there screaming and screaming.

"It was the mouse that made her roar," said Whitaker.

17. Fly In to Fly Fish

Chances are that anywhere fishermen can go by automobile in Alaska, it will be fairly crowded. Truly passionate fishermen who have large bank accounts, however, are willing to spend hundreds of dollars to fly to a remote stream or river for the pleasure of solo fishing. Or at least fishing where the main company is bears.

Brian Kraft, who gained renown in Alaska as a collegiate and professional hockey player, is one guide who caters to the fisherman who would rather be lonely. He established a fishing operation in Bristol Bay, on the Kvichak River and other smaller tributaries. Sometimes he takes a dozen people fishing for salmon, rainbow trout, or grayling. And sometimes he takes just one person at a time.

One of Kraft's favorite customers is a man named George Halper, a gentleman in his thirties from Chicago, Kraft's original home town.

"He was just starting to fall in love with fishing," said Kraft, who watched the angler's enthusiasm grow as he hooked king salmon and rainbow trout.

On about the third day of Halper's trip, a hot, sunny afternoon, the two of them were in a boat. The stream was very narrow and the water was very clear. The men could see the fish swimming past as Kraft rowed.

"We would actually say, 'Oh, there's a big one,'" said Kraft.

Halper hooked a fish and as he fought it, the boat drifted into a whirlpool. There was a log jam, too.

"I'm rowing the boat and the river took a hard turn left,"

said Kraft. "But I couldn't get the fish to turn left. The fish went under the boat and he said, 'What do I do? What do I do?'"

The current was forcing the boat into the logs so it was hard to control, and the boat couldn't be used to advantage to reel in the fish.

"Finally, he goes, 'Oh hell, I'm going in,'" said Kraft.

Halper was wearing shorts and it was warm out, so he figured, "What the heck." He just jumped out of the boat, ducked beneath it, and surfaced on the other side, rod in hand, still fighting the fish, only from a better angle.

The fight goes on and on and the fish still isn't cooperating.

"He's just about to land the fish and he goes, 'Brian, hold my rod. I've got to take a leak.'"

Kraft freaked out. What? Hold the rod? After all that?

Kraft refused to take the rod, deciding if he lost the fish, the fisherman would never forgive him. At long last, Halper reeled in the fish and it was a beauty, a 26-inch rainbow trout. He admired the fish briefly and then let it go.

Another guide whose fishermen must undertake serious travel efforts to come to him is Jerry Austin. A popular musher in the Iditarod Trail Sled Dog Race, he has long worked as a hunting and fishing guide on grounds just south of his home in the tiny western Alaska community of St. Michael, far from the road system.

This is a remote and pristine area, and if a fisherman is coming from the Lower 48, chances are he flies by jet into Anchorage and then either takes a jet to Nome and a small plane to St. Michael, or stops in Unalakleet on the shore of the Bering Sea.

It's a long trip, and this is definitely wilderness territory. When clients show up from South Africa or India, they are impressed.

"They've never seen anything like it," said Austin. "They've never been fishing anywhere where there is no one else on the river."

Several species of salmon pass through the area and they are usually caught from the bank or sand bars, not from boats.

"I've caught a 50-pound king salmon in a little, tiny creek," said Austin. "Lots of big ones get lost on the bank, though. The trick to fishing from shore is just playing them very gently."

The overanxious angler can become a casualty of a flying hook if that advice is not followed.

"I had a twelve- or thirteen-year-old girl from California hooked in the lip," said Austin. "She went into shock. She was reeling in too fast, the rod was not bent over, and the hook just nailed her in the lip. If the lure comes out of the fish's mouth, it just comes straight back at you. All of a sudden, it's Dr. Jerry. She was absolutely fine afterwards."

Most such wounded clients go right back to fishing, said Austin. Not only did they pay a lot of money for a vacation, but where are they going to go? They can't just jump in the car and drive to a hospital.

It actually comes as a surprise to many people, including Alaskans, that king salmon can be caught in areas almost as far north as the Arctic Circle. Perhaps because the Kenai River, the Mat-Su Valley, and the Gulkana River get all the king publicity.

George Bell, in his sixties, now lives in Fairbanks, but he used to fish in Nome and Kotzebue, in the Nome River and the Unalakleet River, and different species of salmon were plentiful, he said.

"Thirty-pound kings were common," he said. "You get out on the Bering Sea coast and they're all good-sized. And you are by yourself. If you see another fisherman within a mile or two, you feel like you've been encroached on.

"I used to go ptarmigan hunting, and while I was out I caught pike. We caught pike up the kazoo. They look too much like a snake for me, though. I gave them to people who need something to eat."

There are so many great fishing places in Alaska that sometimes an angler can accidentally stumble upon a usually crowded place when there's no one around. That happened to Pete Hardy, a state employee who is nicknamed "The Halibut Guru" because of his affinity for halibut fishing. One time, Hardy stopped to fish Goose Creek, north of Anchorage. He was angling for trout on a crisp September day when the leaves were turning.

"I had the place to myself," said Hardy. "I caught two 6-pounders, two 5-pounders, two fours, and umpteen twos and threes. It was just one of those incredible days. It was one of those days that goes down with a bookmark in your mind."

Hardy is a great believer in the cyclical nature of fishing. Some days are going to be horrible, and bad things will occur to make you wish you'd stayed home. And some days are going to be so terrific you will never forget them.

One of Hardy's unfortunate days occurred on a visit to the Anchor River, outside of Homer. It was just past midnight on a Memorial Day weekend.

"I hooked into a fish immediately," said Hardy. "I'm walking up and down the shore in the dark, trying to control the fish, and I hear a snap. Someone had laid his rod down on the path. I had stepped on it and broken it. But I had a fish on and wanted to land it. The fish led me away and I said, 'I'll be back to pay for it.'"

Hardy fought the fish for a half hour and then he released it because it was hooked in the fin. It was a 40-pound king salmon, too.

No fish and he owed another angler for his ruined equipment.

"It cost me twenty-five dollars for the rod," said Hardy. "It was weird."

Scott McDaniel of Anchorage had better luck. In 1986, he caught a 70-pound king salmon on his birthday.

Fishing Sheep Creek, north of the community of Houston, McDaniel was fishing on a fine day with his granddaughter, who has the same June 26 birthdate. He was fishing from the bank, and this was a fish so large it was tough to land. McDaniel needed reinforcements to get it.

"It was a fifty-five-minute fight," said McDaniel, "and it took two nets to bring it in. One was my son-in-law's and another guy helped out. It felt like a log. I was glad to see it on the beach."

After the fish was cut open, McDaniel got another surprise. It was a white king salmon, more common in Southeast Alaska.

"I said, 'It's a what?'" said McDaniel.

The meat of the king was white, as opposed to the normal red meat.

There is good luck and there is bad luck when it comes to fishing, and neither is predictable.

Leonard Patton of Bethel, Alaska, remembers going fishing

with his uncle when he was sixteen years old. A contest was going on that awarded two round-trip tickets to Hawaii for the biggest king salmon caught. They caught a king and weighed it at 82 pounds. Only Leonard's uncle never bothered to bring it to contest officials.

"Nah, there's a bigger one," Patton remembers him saying.

Turns out the winning king salmon weighed 77 pounds.

Another time Patton was fishing on the Kuskokwim River, and the fish were biting insanely.

"I caught two hundred pike in two and a half hours," said Patton. "They didn't last long, either. They tasted good."

Ken Marsh, the former outdoors editor of *Alaska* magazine, has fished all over the huge state. And for just about every kind of fish, too. Once Marsh pursued steelhead, a fish that resembles salmon, in Prince William Sound.

"They're kind of sea run rainbow trout," said Marsh. "They think they're salmon so they get real big. I caught a big one. I called it 37 inches, even though it was 36½ inches. You always round up."

That could well be the fisherman's creed.

"Unlike salmon, they spawn more than once and go back to the ocean and get bigger," said Marsh. "They're very mysterious fish. The biggest one I ever caught was 42 pounds. The average I've caught is 8 to 10 pounds. They fight like crazy."

Fishing is perhaps Marsh's biggest passion in life, but even he can get discouraged by Alaska weather. He remembers fishing on the Goodnews River, southwest of Dillingham, and it was cold and pouring rain.

"It was near snow," he said. "That kind of cold, misty rain. It was deplorable weather."

When he writes stories about fishing, said Marsh, he knows readers think everywhere he goes is idyllic. And these places are—on the right days. On this particular day, Marsh's mood was different.

"I'm thinking, 'I'm going to be happy if I survive this,'" said Marsh. "'Why don't I take cooking classes and become a restaurant critic?'"

Even if Marsh thought the bad weather was driving him

crazy, he would have to admit that he was better off than someone who really was crazy. A story told by people who don't want their names attached to it has made the rounds in Alaska.

It goes like this:

In about 1985 a patient walked away from a psychiatric institution in Anchorage, but eventually the sputtering person was fished out of the Susitna River. According to officials, the patient said that he had taken the train north from Anchorage to Talkeetna and disembarked. Then he had jumped in the river and was swimming along because he wanted to follow the salmon.

See? Everyone in Alaska has salmon fever.

18. A Brash Money-Back Guarantee

In what may be the most unusual Alaska fishing pledge of all time, the Booth family of the Mat-Su Valley has made a virtually unprecedented offer to Alaska fishermen. If you go fishing with them as your guides, they guarantee that you will catch fish.

Stop right there. Fish guaranteed. Really. We're not making this up.

Among fishing guides, 99.9 percent use the phrase, "We don't guarantee fish. We only guarantee that you will have a good time."

That's because nobody can guarantee fish and stay in business. Fish rarely make such bargains with anglers, given that it's their lives at stake.

But meet the .1 percent. The Booths went out on a limb. Actually, all the way to the end of a limb.

Brothers Bill and David Booth got the bright idea to offer a money-back guarantee to fishing clients because the silver salmon fishing on the Little Susitna River, near Talkeetna, was running so strong in the early 1990s.

"On the Little Su, if you don't catch silvers there's something wrong," said David.

Apparently, the brothers believe in the adage "The family that guides together, sticks together." But they are brothers, so they still wanted to one-up each other. Each brother sought to be the one whose clients caught the most fish.

"We're real competitive," said Bill Booth.

Not only with each other. But with other guide services and with the fish.

One day it dawned on them that just about every fisherman who was out with them was catching fish.

"We were bragging about it a couple of years ago," said David.

Bragging like, "My fishermen caught more fish than yours. Nyah, nyah."

This went on for some time. Fisherman after fisherman caught fish with the Booths. The brothers started joking that they could practically guarantee people fish. And then one day they stopped joking about it and David said, "Let's make it official."

The guarantee was born during the summer of 1996.

And the Booth motto was created: "If you don't catch fish, you don't pay."

Pretty catchy and pretty eye-catching.

"A hundred bucks is a lot of money to go fishing," said David Booth. "You need to do your best for them."

Certainly, the incentive is there for the guide service. It's hard to make a profit if you take people fishing for free.

And what about all those other guides who say that if fishermen go fishing with them they're guaranteed a good time?

"The way we look at it, if they say they had a good time and they didn't catch fish, they're lying," said David.

Living dangerously, since king salmon are not as plentiful as silvers, the Booths began the 1996 season by offering a money-back guarantee on catching king salmon. The trips cost $200.

"You don't reel in, you don't pay," said Bill.

However, for whatever reason, nobody took the Booths up on the offer during the king season. Perhaps anglers didn't believe the advertising, or because the arrangement was so new, they didn't hear about it.

By mid-summer, though, when the silvers began running, word had spread. The idea finally caught on. The Booths' eighteen-foot boats were filled with four anglers at a time all the time.

The silver season began well, with fishermen catching fish, but sure enough, one angler came home empty-handed. Instead of taking a refund, though, the man chose to go fishing again, and this time he caught fish. In fact, the man went out fishing three more times and caught fish on every occasion.

Remarkably, everyone else who was fishing with the Booths also caught fish. Angler after angler. Men and women, boys and girls, oldsters and youngsters. The Booths' instincts were correct. They could catch fish for anybody and everybody. They went a month straight without a miss, without having to pay up. Approximately 250 people went fishing for silvers with the Booths that month and every single angler caught fish.

Call the *Guinness Book of World Records*.

There's no doubt the Booths felt the pressure was on them to produce while they were out on the river. Think of the rotten publicity if they made such a bold offer and then failed to live up to it. It wouldn't have been any fun at all to be handing hundred-dollar bills back to clients at the end of each day.

"You turn one guy away, that's bad for business," said Bill. "But if it brings us half as much business again, it's worth it."

And when it works, the word of mouth is terrific. Imagine fishermen running around telling their friends about these crazy guides who guarantee fish—and then come through. How did they do it?

"Hard work is what it is," said David.

Hard work? That's not really a secret formula. Most guides work pretty hard. Certainly, some luck is involved, but just as clearly luck alone won't bring you fish. If so, everyone in Alaska who ever bought a fishing license would run right out to the store and buy a rabbit's foot as well.

The biggest silver caught during this streak of salmon fishing weighed sixteen pounds. That's a keeper, for sure, a trophy silver for some. The Booths admit that the silver run was exceptional during that summer and the conditions of really low water because of a low snow year might not always be matched. So it's possible circumstances beyond their control will be created to prevent the automatic catching of fish in other years.

As if the audacity of making the offer wasn't notable enough, as if the streak of having almost every one of the 250 anglers catch fish wasn't enough, there was one more aspect of the Booths' 1996 summer that was even more amazing.

"The limit is three silvers," said Bill Booth. "I think all but one or two or so caught their limit."

Caught their limit? Where do we sign up?

"We thought we could probably guarantee limits," said Bill, though that idea was re-thought. "We just caught a lot of fish. Ultimately, it's a heck of a lot more fun being out on the river when you reel one in."

Guarantee limits? That would push fishing on The Last Frontier to a new frontier.

19. Thar She Blows!

When you really stop to think about it, it's amazing that anyone lands a major halibut. The immense flatfish can easily weigh 300 pounds and up. If you have ever lifted a fifty-pound box of books and carried it down the hall, you know what a strain that can be. So imagine what kind of workout your arms and shoulders get, even with the leveraging system of a fishing rod and reel.

Still, even with the advantages of technology, there is no guarantee you can bring in the big white fish.

In the summer of 1996, fishing guide Richard Baker had an eighty-year-old Catholic priest on board his vessel outside of Homer, the halibut fishing community that likes to bill itself as the United States' "end of the road" because of its location on the water some 230 miles south of Anchorage.

The man had just returned to the United States from Africa, had just retired, and was on vacation. He was old and a bit frail, so Baker rigged him up with an electric reel as an asset to fight the fish. He also strapped the man into a harness to give him a little more support, so he wouldn't hurt his back if a big fish struck.

Well, four hours into the trip, the big fish did strike. When Baker had his head turned.

"All of a sudden, I hear this thud," said Baker. "The guy comes flying across the boat at Mach 20. He had one hand on the rod and one hand on the rail. He was hanging on for dear life. He was scared to death."

A two-minute struggle that seemed like two hours ensued

between man and fish. Only this was no halibut. The priest had hooked a 5-foot-long, 300-hundred-pound porpoise, and it stripped the line right off the electric reel. So much for extra power.

"We cut the line, let the porpoise go, and saved the old man," said Baker. "If that doesn't get me into heaven, nothing will."

The size of the porpoise was impressive, but 300-pound halibut are certainly available. Those are the trophy fish of the breed and in Alaska are commonly termed "barn door" halibut because of their width and flatness. Face it, halibut are not pretty creatures by human standards. They could be a throw-rug with eyes. But they make good eating, and hunting them down makes for good adventures.

Guide Steve Morphus has a fiberglass mount of a 350-pound halibut that he totes around for special occasions like the Great Alaska Sportsman Show in Anchorage. The rest of the time it lives in storage in Homer.

"It takes up about half the garage," said Morphus, who said the halibut was caught by an Anchorage woman a few years ago in Cook Inlet. "It about yanked her over the side of the boat. It took her about three hours to bring it in. She was tired, but she was happy."

Showing off the mount itself is good for business, he believes, but it is fragile and, while huge, it is not made up of flesh and bone.

"She takes her one trip to Anchorage a year," said Morphus. "She only weighs twenty pounds. It would float. It could surf."

The most renowned halibut fishing grounds are in the waters off Homer. Far off Homer, perhaps forty to sixty miles. The thousands of fishermen who take charter trips each summer start out at about five o'clock in the morning, sailing through Kachemak Bay, and often don't return to land for twelve to fourteen hours. Typical group sizes are a half-dozen on so-called "six-pack" boats and a dozen or more on larger boats. These are neither rafts nor the sixteen-foot, aluminum-hulled boats used on rivers like the Kenai. These are seafaring ships designed to withstand the chop of big waves.

The length of the day, the toil, and the effort required for halibut fishing catches some people by surprise.

"The biggest thing most people are not ready for is the strenuous nature of halibut fishing," said guide Rod Berg. "You're getting hit all the time fishing heavy currents in Cook Inlet."

In sunny weather, the journey offshore can be stunningly beautiful. Mountains stand tall in the distance, the water is blue and glistening, and visitors are in awe of the scenery.

"They look at the mountains and get a puzzled look on their faces and ask how far above sea level we are," said Berg.

His response? Berg raises his hand to the top of his forehead as if saluting and says, "This far."

Captain Dave Mastolier of Lucky Pierre Charters says the same thing happens to him and calls the "How far are we above sea level?" line his favorite dumb question.

"I was in shock," said Mastolier. "Some people thought they were on a lake. We were saltwater fishing. I guess they thought they were on the Great Salt Lake."

Mastolier sometimes gets in a mischievous mood. In the Barren Islands, where he normally fishes for halibut, about sixty miles from Homer, Mastolier points to the mountains and says, "That's Russia."

The clients shoot pictures, then later Mastolier tells them the truth.

As is generally true with most types of fishing, there is no hard-and-fast rule about appropriate bait. Certain things seem to work with more frequency, but there's no way to be sure what will be appetizing on a given day.

"About six years ago I had a woman out with me from out of state," said Mastolier. "She caught a 130-pound halibut. Good for her. She was happy. The tide was running hard and she decided to take a break. She ate a snack, a chicken leg. Then she tied the bone to the hook for bait, threw it overboard, and promptly caught a 170-pounder."

There are periodic stories about fishing rods going overboard on the Kenai River and later being caught by other fishermen, but if a rod is lost on the high seas you can pretty much forget about it. Which is why one Berg tale is so incredible.

"We lost a rod overboard in pretty deep water," said Berg of the incident when a fisherman on one of his other captains' boats put a rod down to reach for a sandwich, only to have a fish choose that moment to take his bait.

"I thought that one was gone. About two weeks later the same skipper hooked into the rod and brought it up. The reel is still a basket case. It was all rusty. I never did try to rebuild it."

The size of a halibut alone does not always strictly produce a correlation with the length of the battle to land it.

Captain Bob, a Homer guide since 1991, said in his experience a halibut weighing 250 pounds will come to papa easier than a lighter weight one.

"Bigger ones come in easier than the small ones," said Captain Bob. "They're lazy. If you weighed 250 pounds, you'd be lazy, too."

He remembers a 60-pounder fighting with a fury.

"Fishermen thought they had a monster, and it took forty or fifty minutes to bring it in," said Captain Bob. "And then they said, 'Where's the rest of it?'"

When you are dealing with the murky waters of the deep, there are going to be cases of mistaken identity as well.

Peter Udelhoven of Silver Fox Charters has a personal best halibut catch of 326 pounds, but in the summer of 1996, fishing at Bluff Point in Kachemak Bay, he thought one of his people might have a monumental king salmon on the line.

"I thought we had a tremendous salmon on," said Udelhoven. "I thought it might even be a new world record. We messed around for an hour. Finally, it surfaced and we saw what it was—a six-foot-long harbor seal. Maybe next time. You never know."

The guiding principle of business is that the customer is always right. But in guiding, that guideline doesn't always apply if one insufferable client makes life painful for everyone else. What do you do, drop him overboard? The temptation might be there, but that's probably not a practical approach, so alternative solutions must be found.

Bob Candopoulos of Saltwater Safari said he once had a very aggravating client on board for a trip on Seward's Resurrection Bay.

"He was a Texan who owned his own business," said

Candopoulos. "He was arrogant, loud, and he brought his own little entourage."

The moment he stepped on the boat, Candopoulos sensed trouble because the man announced, "I only deal in sure bets. I expect to catch a fish."

Candopoulos reproved him, saying, "In this business, there are no guarantees."

About two hours into the trip, the man hooked up with a big fish, which, judging by the fight, Candopoulos guessed might be a 200-pound halibut. However, when the guide tried to coach the client so he could land it, the man ignored him and teased him.

"The captain says this. The captain says that," the man said. Then he took one hand off the rod to pose for pictures by the boat rail. And after thirty minutes of this type of activity, naturally he lost the fish.

All of the man's friends and co-workers were catching fish and he wasn't, so he got disgusted and went below decks to take a nap.

An irritated Candopoulos decided the angler should be taught a lesson. So while the man slept, Candopoulos took a large and quite heavy sea anchor, attached it to his rod, and dropped it into the current about three hundred feet deep. Everybody played along and yelled, "Fish on!" to wake up the man.

"He grabs the rod," said Candopoulos, "and he's very excited. He says, 'Okay, I'll pay attention. I know I screwed up before.'"

As the man played the "fish," the guide played the client, telling him he did this wrong before and that wrong before. And he boosted the stature of the big catch, telling him it was bigger than any other fish they'd ever had.

Needless to say, the catch wasn't coming in. After thirty-five minutes, Candopoulos consulted his watch, took out a knife, and cut the line.

"'The only guarantee I can give you is that at five o'clock, we go in,'" he told the man. "He went berserk."

Jim Blake of Break Time Charters remembers the time about

a decade ago when he and his male deckhands got super excited at the sight of the six babes walking down the dock intending to come out fishing with them. All these sexy blondes from Sweden. Ooh-la-la.

The pros couldn't wait to help the frail flowers up close and personal when they caught a big fish. Only the call for assistance never came.

"As the day wore on, things just weren't adding up," said Blake. "Somewhere along the line we realized things weren't what we thought. They all caught fish and we noticed their strength. They didn't really need our help."

The anglers were all transsexuals.

"They all used to be guys," said Blake.

There is one universal commonality among just about all halibut fishing guides who prowl Alaska waters: They are superstitious about bananas. It is strictly forbidden to bring bananas aboard. If you do, bad things will happen, or bad fishing will result.

No one can pinpoint the origin of this superstition, but it has a strong grip on captains. Most captains ask clients if they have bananas with them for a snack and if they do, ask them to get rid of them. Some resort to search and seizure. If bananas are spied when the ship is at sea, usually they are just hurled overboard. No one wants to be jinxed.

Blake is an unabashed extremist on the subject.

"You need to check for bananas," said Blake. "You've got to look in the cooler. Sometimes they'll lie to you. You might laugh at it, but whenever a banana slips by, something breaks or someone drops a camera. And it usually happens to the person who has the bananas."

Although 99 percent of all fishermen seek the biggest halibut they can possibly catch, once Lucky Pierre's Mastolier had a group out that only wanted smaller halibut. They apparently just didn't want to deal with having that much fish in the freezer. Since they only wanted to catch fish weighing under 40 pounds, Mastolier figured he had it made, that it would definitely be an easy charter for fulfillment.

"So of course, they couldn't miss," said Mastolier. "They

caught nothing under 40. The biggest was 303 pounds. They traded it for a 15-pounder. That's the darndest thing I've ever seen."

Sometimes frequency of hits makes up for smallness of size.

"Sometimes you wait and nothing happens," said Mastolier. "And sometimes things just go crazy."

He calls the day when just that occurred while fishing in the Barren Islands the equivalent of a small-scale riot.

"We caught thirty fish in two hours," he said. "We could only fish six people at a time. It was, 'Who hasn't caught a fish yet?' It was that fast."

There was another boat fishing the grounds about twenty feet away and not a single strike was made by that group.

"Finally they pulled up closer and said, 'We can't take it anymore,'" said Mastolier. "Everyone was in shock. There were lines all over the place. There were twelve adults fishing.

"It was very entertaining. And we had bananas on the boat. I always say it's a good excuse for a captain when he had a bad catch. People were standing there eating bananas watching the fish being brought in."

Yeah, but next time out those people probably slipped on a banana peel and fell overboard.

20. Sometimes It's Easier to Talk to the Fish

Homer Ocean Charter fishing guide Rick Swenson, who shares the same name as the famous Iditarod Trail Sled Dog Race champion, had one of the great high seas misunderstandings of all time in 1990. This one rates high on the embarrassment meter.

Swenson is no linguist and maybe he's lucky, given what happened on the day he took six people halibut fishing on his six-passenger boat. With him were four Pennsylvania Dutch, only one of whom spoke English, and two Koreans, neither of whom spoke English.

"That was the mix for the day," said Swenson, who admitted his Korean is limited. "I can bow. That's it."

The women in the Pennsylvania Dutch contingent wore traditional garb, including head coverings and big, black, billowing skirts.

It was a weird day from the start, with the toilet overflowing and the weather turning nasty and producing rough seas on Cook Inlet that tossed everyone around uncomfortably.

Someone caught a small halibut and brought it in. The fish lay on the deck, and Swenson was down on one knee trying to remove the hook as waves buffeted the boat. The force knocked one of the Pennsylvania Dutch women off-balance. She fell over onto Swenson and her skirt flew up over her head, fanning out and covering Swenson's head.

"It goes totally dark," he said.

He was underneath her skirt, still gripping the 20-pound halibut, which had not quite been subdued.

"It decides to come alive," said Swenson. "We end up in a heap on the deck."

Pandemonium. People are yelling, flailing, pulling at Swenson and the woman, and the boat is rolling and tilting.

"Everyone is talking a mile a minute, and I have no idea what everyone's saying," said Swenson.

It took a few minutes to disengage. When everything was straightened out and everybody calmed down, the one man in the Pennsylvania Dutch group who spoke English stared solemnly at Swenson and said, "We are ready to go home now."

Needless to say, there were no repeat customers from that trip.

One major difference between halibut fishing in places like Kachemak Bay off Homer and Resurrection Bay off Seward, and salmon fishing in places like the Kenai River is the comparative likelihood of seasickness. People don't get ill on the rivers. They sometimes do on the ocean.

Ted Raynor has a theory about that, though. The guide for Homer Charters said even if someone throws up, they consider the trip a success if they bring home fish.

"If they catch a lot of fish, they don't care how hard they're retching," said Raynor. "They're smiling ear to ear."

Once Swenson had some flight attendants fishing with him, and one woman had long blond hair that reached down below her waist. She was feeling terrible, leaning over the rail, crying. At the last minute, before she heaved, Swenson pulled her hair out of the way.

Another time he was out with the CEO of a major corporation and his wife. The man got sick and his wife, watching over him, reached out and pinched his butt.

Then there was the occasion when Swenson thought he had lost a man overboard.

The anglers consisted of five brothers from Minnesota, all professional men, doctors, dentists, lawyers, all in their fifties and sixties. After a two-day delay because of bad weather in Homer, they finally got out on the water. But after just an hour and a half of fishing, there was a sudden clamor. Only four of them were in sight. One brother was missing.

"I was just talking to him," said one brother.

"Panic sets in," said Swenson. "These guys are just distraught."

Swenson wondered what to do. He couldn't imagine how he lost someone at sea. He turned the boat around and started to retrace their path back to shore. Next, he flipped on his radio and phoned home—to the office. When he got through to the operator and reported the missing man, he was told, "He was just here five minutes ago."

It turned out that the fifth brother had dashed to the bathroom just as the boat was to leave and missed the departure.

"So we went fishing," said Swenson.

Some fishermen have magical luck. Once Sean Martin of North Country Charters in Homer had a group fishing off Anchor Point. One man had never been halibut fishing before, and he hooked into a big one.

"We figured it must be 600 pounds by the way it went," said Martin. "I thought it would spool the rod in two minutes. A deckhand dragged it up with 80-pound test line."

That kind of rope is about as thick as anchor chain.

However, the fish was hooked in the tail and that's why it was so tough to bring in.

"We pulled it up sideways and harpooned it in the head," said Martin. "It was hooked on just a quarter-inch of skin. It was unbelievable it held."

The halibut weighed 219 pounds.

And the fortunate fisherman? A little while later he caught a 35-pound king salmon as a bonus.

"We catch about one king a year," said Martin.

Charley Brown of Charley Charters had an instant response when he was asked what the strangest thing was that ever happened to him while halibut fishing.

"I hooked a whale," he said.

One man on his boat hooked a halibut and Brown was helping him. Brown noticed a pilot whale in the near distance. Then he took hold of the rod of the kid fishing nearby to move it out of harm's way.

"As soon as I get it, Boom!" he said. "It stripped off three hundred yards of line. I had no idea what it was. This thing was going out faster than you can throw a rock."

Within moments the line snapped. Brown said he never

actually saw the whale, which was probably 30 feet long and weighed tons, on the line, but is convinced that's what it was because of the previous sighting.

A few years ago, one of Brown's crew caught a sea lion. There was a halibut on a line and the sea lion surfaced chomping on the halibut.

Raynor said people have caught three-foot squid.

"They're extremely aggressive," he said. "They spray you. They have real powerful water jets and they ink all over the place."

Keith Washburn of Fantasea Charters once brought in a halibut that topped 315 pounds, and it was quite an adventure. He was fishing on Resurrection Bay in sight of the Seward docks in August 1995, but this was one fish that under the strictest of definitions never could quite be landed.

"It was too heavy," said Washburn. "Its head would hit the railing every time. We couldn't get it over the side and had to rig it up to tow it back to shore. That fish won me a $250 dinner and cost me a thousand dollars to catch."

As Washburn's boat towed the fish to shore, a man fell off the dock into the water. Right in front of them. Washburn put the boat into reverse instead of docking. When he did so, the fish got caught in the propellers, which sucked up that fish's tail. The fish beat up the propeller and messed up the cutlass bearing, doing a thousand dollars worth of damage.

Washburn was rewarded with a nice dinner for the catch, so all in all figures it was worth it.

"I got a thousand dollars worth of bragging rights from the story," said Washburn.

Washburn, who has been guiding for fifteen years, had a scare once when a fisherman with him caught a 215-pounder. He strained and tugged and landed it.

"He was so excited he was having seizures on deck," said Washburn. "He told me he had a medical retirement. As he was bringing it up, he told me it was because of heart problems."

The man survived.

Several years ago, Washburn was surprised to find himself officiating at a wedding. His wife had booked the trip and told

Washburn, "You're going to do it." A young couple from Anchorage said they wanted to get married on a fishing trip and said since he was a captain, he could do it.

Washburn went to the State of Alaska offices and researched his powers and found out he could indeed perform a marriage. They told him he could do it up to six times a year, he said.

So the wedding was held on Resurrection Bay. The couple wrote out the ceremony's wording.

"We haven't done any burials at sea," said Washburn. "We've had some that needed it."

Washburn says one of the fun things about being a fishing guide is the mix of people he meets. He's had visitors fishing from all over the world, from perhaps twenty countries. But nothing quite matched the time in the early 1990s when he booked a fishing trip for two separate groups of people. One group were hard-core environmentalists. Another couple consisted of a commercial logger and his wife.

"It was cats and dogs, oil and water," said Washburn. "It didn't get violent, but it got ugly when the environmentalists forcefully expressed their views. That was one day I was happy to get done."

Once you're out on the water, you're in for a ten-hour day or longer, so you hope to make the best of it no matter who is fishing. There was no making the best of it, though, with the client Washburn nicknamed "Bud Man."

He came on board carrying two twelve-packs of beer. He drank one entire pack while he was fishing during the day and then he finished off the second one in about fifteen minutes back at the dock.

"Then he got obnoxious," said Washburn. "You don't argue with a guy with a twelve-inch filet knife."

Washburn called the police.

Then there was the famous anonymously told story about a time when the police might have been called. On a six-person charter boat, the skipper was carrying a .44. The gun was out on the table. A speech was made about avoiding accidents. And on cue, the gun went off in the cabin. The bullet traveled across the table, up the wall, across the ceiling, and back down the other wall.

Everyone lived to tell about it, though no one wanted to.

Bill Jones of Admiral Charters has been guiding out of Seward since 1984 and the biggest single-day catch he ever had was 1,251 pounds of halibut for four people. Tons of fish for dinner. Hold the potatoes.

He claims he once caught a 400-pound halibut but couldn't find a scale big enough to weigh it. He has a videotape of a 300-pounder caught on his boat that led pursuers on a ten-mile chase for ninety minutes.

"People say halibut don't run," said Jones. "They don't know what they're talking about. Halibut generally don't run more than a hundred yards at a time and then they take a breath. I had to crank up the boat and run him down. The fisherman was excited and worn out, I'll tell you."

Needed an arm rub.

He's not the only angler that's happened to, of course. Raynor remembers the time he had a woman in her seventies out fishing with him and when she tried to reel in a good-sized halibut it left her quite weary.

"It felt like an elephant," she said.

It takes elbow grease to land the biggest halibut.

"We've hooked some you couldn't even do anything with," said Raynor. "It leaves you shaking and feeling like jelly. It seems like time slows down when you're doing something like that."

Perhaps intervention of a higher power is warranted. Jones, the Admiral Charter boss, might be able to speak to that matter.

For some reason, for a little while Jones's halibut charters attracted men of the clergy. One Sunday he had a whole group out with him. They fished hard all day and couldn't catch anything.

"I said, 'God's punishing you for not being in church,'" said Jones.

On a different day Jones had a solo preacher with him. The man hooked a fish and said, "Oh, God."

Jones had a quip ready.

"I said, 'Preacher, are you prayin' or cussin'?'"

21. Fish the Size of Football Players

John Nicholson is a former Oklahoma University football player in his early fifties who has been fishing for halibut off Homer for seventeen years. A guy who would make a good-sized halibut catch himself, Nicholson has brought in some of the largest flatfish of all.

In the summer of 1997, an angler fishing with the Ultimate Charters captain did discover close to the ultimate halibut and bring it home. Mike Pearson of Sutton, Alaska, was planning to buy a Homer Jackpot Halibut Derby ticket on his way to the boat, but his car broke down. So he didn't have time before disembarking to enter the rich-paying annual contest for the largest halibut caught.

Too bad since Pearson landed a halibut fishing with Nicholson that weighed in at just under 420 pounds. Which was larger than any football player Nicholson might have encountered in his youth. The world-record halibut belongs to Jack Tragis, who caught a 459-pounder in Dutch Harbor, Alaska (of course), in 1996. Both of those behemoth fish dwarf The Fridge or any other National Football League lineman.

"It felt like a pickup truck hit my line," said Pearson, who was fishing in the popular Barren Islands area and fought the fish for more than an hour before declaring victory.

Nicholson has had good fishing fortune before. On a 1991 trip, he said his group of Alaska clients caught 3,400 pounds of halibut in four hours.

"We found a big old pile of fish," said Nicholson. "The next morning I made the mistake of trying to go back there. At five o'clock in the morning, the area was mobbed. It was like *The Hunt for Red October."*

Vessels everywhere sounding the deep.

Nicholson, who doesn't mind celebrating big catches with a beer or two, remembers the occasion when well-known Alaskan crooner Hobo Jim was performing in Homer and he felt compelled to join him on stage and sing along.

"Then I yelled, 'How many people are going halibut fishing tomorrow?'" said Nicholson.

About 150 people raised their hands.

"I told them they were stupid," said Nicholson, "that it was going to be windy, with high tides."

Somehow he survived the night in the bar, though it did end his career as a weather forecaster since the next day it was flat calm on the ocean.

Because the seas can be choppy, those who are prone to seasickness are advised to take it easy on the intake of goodies while sailing. When Nicholson saw one tourist chowing down on jalapeño dip, he had a sense of foreboding.

"Guaranteed to get you sick," said Nicholson. "He started turning green. The rest of the day he was on his knees."

Several years ago, Nicholson made news in the Anchorage papers by catching tons of halibut with a bevy of attractive flight attendants. On three different trips, they averaged catches of between 2,400 and 2,700 pounds, all caught within twenty-five miles of the Homer dock.

At the time he was dating one of the young ladies, but they all had such a good time fishing that when he broke up with her, the others asked if they could still come fishing.

"I said, 'Hell, no,'" said Nicholson.

One of Nicholson's favorite regulars was an older gentleman, a postman from Oregon who had to save his pennies to afford trips to Alaska.

"He just loved halibut fishing," said Nicholson. "He caught a 90-pounder and a 190-pounder. He had tears in his eyes the last time he came. He said, 'John, I just can't afford it anymore.'"

One of the oldest anglers Nicholson ever took halibut fishing was eighty-six, and he left Nicholson shaking.

"He had a pacemaker and we were fishing, and all of a sudden, he hits the deck," said Nicholson. "I think, 'Oh boy, I finally killed someone.'"

But the man's son piped up and said he was all right, it's just that sometimes his father's heart got out of synch.

"It happened twice," said Nicholson. "Talk about scary."

The man lay down for a while, then went back to fishing.

"He got fish that day, one that weighed 70 or 80 pounds," said Nicholson. "He was from California, and he died that winter."

Another time someone really did die at sea on a Nicholson trip.

"He was a forty-seven-year-old paraplegic diabetic, and he had a massive heart attack," said Nicholson. "He had to be medivaced off the boat."

Over the years, Nicholson has seen a twelve-year-old boy who weighed seventy pounds catch a 200-pound halibut. And he has seen a six-foot-five, 250-pound iron worker who had a "Don't get in the way" attitude toward his small wife be outfished by her.

"She gets a big halibut, 230 pounds," said Nicholson. "He was a little bit upset about it. He didn't bring her anymore."

Until Pearson caught the big one with Nicholson, the guide's personal record for largest halibut taken in his boat was 351 pounds nabbed by a man named Bucky Howard, whom Nicholson estimated weighed 350 pounds himself.

"He was asleep in a chair when the fish bit," said Nicholson.

During the 1996 season, Nicholson said he caught a thousand fish that weighed at least a hundred pounds.

"That was a milestone for me," he said.

Even after all this time on the water, Nicholson said he still gets excited when an angler catches a big halibut.

"I still about wet my pants when someone catches one," he said. "I'm more excited than they are."

Part of what Nicholson loves about being a Homer halibut guide is the off-hours camaraderie with other skippers.

Once, said Nicholson, at the end of the season he was with another skipper named Vic at the famed Homer Salty Dawg Saloon drinking, as he put it, "lemonade and iced tea" at 2 A.M.

His office booking agent found him and told him a group of people wanted to fish. There would be two shifts the next day, 7 A.M. to noon, and noon to 6 P.M. Nicholson and Vic flipped a coin for the right to sleep in. Nicholson won.

When Nicholson meandered down to the dock about noon, he found "fifteen angry people and no fish in the box."

The afternoon did not promise improvement. The fishing was nonexistent for most of four hours when Nicholson, out of desperation, took a shot in an unlikely location. All of a sudden, fish turned up and Nicholson's group hauled in many in the 80- to 100-pound range.

When he pulled his boat up to the dock, there was a bleary-eyed Vic.

"Vic," Nicholson sang, "I'm hooommme."

With 1,600 pounds of halibut.

"I had the last laugh," said Nicholson. "Vic left after that and never came back."

22. Don't Turn Your Back

Over the years, Bill Jones of Admiralty Charters has had his share of *Jaws*-type experiences on the ocean.

One day a woman fishing for halibut on his boat caught a ling cod, not a sought-after fish, but one that occasionally takes a swipe at halibut bait.

"She was looking to the other side and when she turned back, a great big shark came up and took the fish," said Jones. "It was a salmon shark, between 12 and 14 feet long. She was hysterical. She had to go sit in the cabin the rest of the day."

Another time an unwelcome bass grabbed the bait and, when the angler started reeling in, a ling cod opened wide and swallowed that fish.

"She looked down and screamed," said Jones. "The ling cod let it go. She scared it."

Not that he's complaining, but Jones remembers the time his thirty-foot boat was floundering from the weight of nine fish weighing between 130 and 200 pounds.

"One more big fish and we'll sink the boat," Jones told his crew. So he turned the boat and ran with the tide for miles.

Jones's son David, who works with him, has a pretty good father-son tale about a different father-and-son combo in the summer of 1994. The eight-year-old boy wanted a big fish in the worst way. He bet his dad five dollars that he would get the bigger fish.

"Dad got one on right away," said David Jones. "But he lost it. Soon the boy was yelling and screaming and his pole was all bent over. The line was running and the pole action made it seem like a huge halibut."

No wonder. He had hooked a humpback whale. The dad somberly said, "Son, I think you should let this one go."

The dad did fork over the five bucks, though. "You beat me," he conceded. "That's going to be hard to beat."

Richard Baker of Alaska Wildlife and Fishing Adventures remembers receiving a reward of a different kind when someone on one of his boats fishing out of Homer caught a 368-pound halibut.

"It comes up pretty easy," he said. "It took a little over an hour to bring in. Everybody was jumping up and down, and I had old ladies pinching my cheek and kissing me."

A few years ago, Baker had a boy and his mother from California fishing. The kid was napping, and all of a sudden an orca whale surfaced by the boat. The boy woke up and sleepily said, "It's Willy."

Meaning the whale in the movie *Free Willy*.

"His mother says, 'No, it's not Willy, is it, Captain?'" said Baker. "I didn't want to get in the middle of that. I said, 'I'm not sure. Who's Willy?'"

Another time, Baker had a senior citizen on board who seemed to be having a stroke.

"All of a sudden, he turns white, then he gets flushed," said Baker. "His wife says, 'He's okay. He does that all the time. Let's just keep fishing. We need to get our limit.'"

Baker said he was muttering under his breath that he hoped the guy didn't die on his boat. As it was, the man did go to the hospital as soon as they docked.

Baker offered a bit of light-hearted advice for anyone who wants to train for halibut fishing.

"Get a Humvee, hook a rope to the back of the car, and tell the driver to go," he said. "And when you can reel it back in, you're ready to go halibut fishing."

Once Baker took out a corps of Marines from Texas. Talk about your machismo quotient.

"They were all puffed up," he said. "There was nobody tougher than them. The first two fish they caught each weighed 100 pounds or more. A colonel caught the first one, and he was so worn out from the heavy lifting he had to go in the cabin and lie down. The others were the same. They were fished out and fatigued. By the end of the day they couldn't lift a beer can up and they were trying."

A 100-pound halibut is notable. A 200-pound halibut is memorable. A 300-pound halibut is a once-in-a-lifetime catch. So what does that make a 400-pounder? Well, you recall every detail.

On June 30, 1992, guide Mel Erickson helped Don Thompson of Tacoma, Washington, catch a 410-pound halibut in 220 feet of water eighteen miles offshore.

"We definitely knew we had something on," said Erickson. "I had never caught one over 300 pounds before. In the water they're magnified. I was saying, 'This one's got to be over 300.'"

They were fishing from a twenty-four-foot boat and had a heck of a time bringing it in. Everyone pulled and pulled and couldn't raise it.

"We finally put a rope around its tail and heaved it over that way," said Erickson. "It was all we could muster."

They harpooned the halibut, they gaffed it, and it took up so much room in the boat the ends of the fish curled up over the sides.

Gary Ault of Inlet Charters once had a group of Korean fishermen out who didn't speak English. His big problem was making them understand that the herring they carried was bait.

"They thought they were fish we were going to keep," he said. "Anything was a keeper. I was just happy they didn't carve up the bait and start eating that."

The trip became just as much fun as fishing with people who did speak English, said Ault. And not nearly as aggravating as being out with anglers who think they know it all.

"Being a guide is a pressure deal," he said. "You don't catch a bunch of fish, and some people think they've gotten screwed. I've had some people say if they don't catch 100 pounds of fish, they won't be back."

Skipper John Armstrong, a former Navy commander who has guided since 1975, developed a personalized halibut fishing philosophy.

Number one, he said, "every trip's different. It's the chemistry, the makeup, and attitude of the people who get on the boat."

Number two, he said, is "All fishermen are liars, except you and me."

Armstrong used to be one of sixty-five sailors attached to Elmendorf Air Force Base. He was always asked what the Navy did in Anchorage, since there was an Air Force base and an Army base, but no Navy base. He was sometimes asked if it was his job to fish, a reasonable question since he surely did pack up and go fishing whenever possible.

"We had a standing order that if anyone was looking for an officer, we said the officer was at 'Annex 1,'" said Armstrong. "That was the code word for the Kenai River." There was also "Annex 2," which meant "on board a riverboat."

Armstrong used to have a regular from Fairbanks who was determined to catch a big halibut even though he always got seasick. This went on for four or five years. He came out on one of his regular trips and as usual "was sicker than a dog all day."

Everyone else on the boat was catching fish, and once more this guy was getting shut out. The weather worsened and Armstrong announced they would pack it up in fifteen minutes.

"He drops a line, and I think this fish hit the bait before it hit the water," said Armstrong.

The man got his big halibut, one that weighed 194 pounds.

"He's never been back since," said Armstrong.

Pete Hardy is no guide, just an Alaskan who loves halibut fishing. His friends gave him the nickname "The Halibut Guru," because he is bald, a little portly, and one day a friend said, "Halibut fishing is like a religion to you, right?" Therefore, he is a guru. Hardy, a state employee, actually now gives halibut-catching seminars.

Hardy's biggest halibut weighed 215 pounds.

"I've had three bigger than that get away," he said. "I've lost them because of gear failures and also brain failure, which is also a gear failure."

One of those lost halibut was so strong it shifted the boat a quarter turn just on the strike.

Dan Schaff of Judy Ann's Charters said that once, in a hundred feet of water at Anchor Point, he had a halibut on the line so powerful it towed the boat five miles towards the Kenai River.

"I was thinking it was a world-record halibut," said Schaff.

And then poof! It was gone. One sharp turn and it broke the line.

"We never saw it," said Schaff. "It wasn't a whale. We assume now it was a shark. We could have given it a good shot."

Some anglers who show up to sit in Schaff's eighteen-foot ocean skiff are clueless about the environment.

"Women show up in high heels," he said. "We have an extra pair of boots for them."

Jim Thompson of Thompson Charters in Homer believes guides must maintain a sense of humor, but he discovered sometimes you have to be careful about your jokes.

"In 1995, I had a seventy-one-year-old lady out with me and she had never fished in her life," said Thompson. "She caught a 301-pound halibut and she was ballistic over this fish."

Thompson's mistake?

"I joked that I was gonna release it and shoot for a bigger fish," he said. "She wasn't in a mood to release that fish."

Actually, Thompson has bigger problems with fishermen who catch small halibut and think they're big ones. They resist throwing them back.

"Many times when the first fish caught is small by halibut standards, people complain that they want to keep it," said Thompson. "They might never have seen a fish as big as 20 pounds. I have a tough time on the first fish of the day. Square-inch-wise, it's the biggest fish they have ever caught.

"I say, 'Let it grow up.' They don't relate to it. I say, 'I think I can do better.' Sometimes I slip and don't talk to them beforehand and they say, 'What have you done to me?'

"Then I say, 'If we're really lucky, we'll increase it ten times.' I have a hard time convincing them. I have had people not speak to me for hours for releasing a halibut that weighed 25 pounds."

Thompson has fished the waters of Cook Inlet since he was ten years old and he's past fifty now. What keeps his guiding job fresh, he said, is the people.

"If you couldn't approach it with a new group of people, you couldn't do this job," he said. "We get doctors from New York and construction workers from New Mexico. They come together and by the end of the day they're on a super first-name basis and relating job stories. It's fun to listen to. They have one thing in common and it's fishing."

23. Tricks of the Trade

Experience shows that Bob Ward's bucket trick works just as well as a practical joke among friends as it does serving as punishment for people who, let us say, may not be feeling quite so warmly about each other.

Some years ago, Ward, who operates A-Ward Charters, had a group of a half-dozen men out fishing for halibut with him in Cook Inlet, south of Homer. Ranging in age from fifty-eight to seventy-five, they were business partners and pals.

On a beautiful day, there was a lot of teasing and joking. When the oldest member of the group, the leader of the pack, went to the bathroom, the others spied a five-gallon, white plastic bucket generally used to wash the deck.

"The guy's rod is in the holder," said Ward, who has long blond hair, a beard, wears a cap, and would look at home as a member of the singing group Z Z Top. "They turned the rope around his line and put it in the water. The current takes it away. It was out of sight."

The bucket sank and sank. When the man returned to his fishing post, he was alerted that he seemed to have a fish on. Twenty seconds later, the rod bent double.

"People start urging him on," said Ward, "talking about how big it must be. All his buddies are teasing him about the big fish. He sat there and reeled and reeled."

Going along, Mr. Guide told the man the fish was so tough to bring in because it was running.

"It's a $30,000 fish," the man was told. "It's going to be the winner," he said, referring to the annual halibut derby.

After almost forty minutes, the angler finally hauled his catch above water line and his first reaction gazing at the gaping chasm of the bucket's top was, "God, look at the mouth on this thing."

The comment reduced everyone else on board to hysterics. The man took being the brunt of the joke well, said Ward, and the joke itself seemed reliable, something that could be tried again.

"I was surprised with how well it worked," said Ward.

Given the successful precedent, Ward did employ the trick again. A year later a group of airline executives were out fishing with him. There were ten anglers, five each in two boats which fished within hailing distance of one another. The underlings were catching all of the choice fish and the boss man was not pleased.

"He was acting annoyed because he felt he had to catch the biggest fish," said Ward.

He kept bugging Ward, and his attitude began to spoil everyone else's good time. The man adjourned to the bathroom and that gave Ward the opportunity to try the bucket stunt once more. Not knowing what was happening at first, the others played along and their silence was considered assent.

The same scenario played out. The man returned from the head and thought he had a fish on. He fought the fish, giving it a heartfelt battle.

"Every once in a while I'd reel the line and pull it tight and he thinks he has a live fish," said Ward. "He's got every indication he's got a big fish. He's totally convinced he's bringing up THE FISH."

This went on for close to an hour, and again the others in the group were ever-helpful, telling the man not to lose the fish, not to let the line rub the edge of the boat. Finally, the "fish" cracked the surface.

"Jesus Christ!" the man exploded. "It's a goddamn bucket!"

There was much teasing, and Ward later learned that when they all returned to work, some of the guys cut a bucket in half and had it mounted on a plaque. Hence, the first trophy bucket.

"He did not take it well," said Ward.

Ward, a guide for twelve years, is assisted by his daughter, Alie, in her early twenties. He pilots the boat *No Problem.* She skippers the boat *Problem*. Both of them seem capable of creating problems for the uncooperative, though.

Sometime in the future, said Ward, he is sure to bring the bucket trick back.

"It will get used again," he said.

Sean Martin of North Country Charters thinks he knows how Captain Ahab felt. Martin had his own whale woes. During the summer of 1996, Martin, a two-decade halibut guide out of Homer, said he was "attacked by a school of juvenile delinquent orcas. They would hover around the boat and steal every halibut we got."

Another time a big humpback whale approached his boat. Martin had sixteen anglers on his fifty-three-foot boat, the *Irish*, when a sixty-foot whale surfaced, trailing a half-dozen of their lines on its pectoral fins.

"He came up to within maybe a hundred feet of the boat," said Martin. "The lines were just burning. I ran up and down cutting the lines. One woman claimed she had caught the whale and told me to slow down and turn back."

Right.

Then there was the time Martin witnessed an "Old Man and the Sea" battle involving a fisherman, a halibut, and a sea lion. The angler caught a 100-pound halibut, only before he could reel it all the way in, a bull sea lion showed up and took a chomp out of it. It was an unequal battle since the sea lion probably weighed 2,000 pounds.

"It was huge," said Martin. "Its head was as big as a beachball. Bigger. We wanted the fish, too."

The fisherman fought hard and got the halibut to within thirty feet of the boat.

"Then the sea lion came back and just shredded the halibut with its teeth," said Martin. "We got the head and little streamers trailing in the water. Then the sea lion came back again. It surfaced, came straight up next to us, and put its head on the boat's back rail, five feet above the water. The fisherman was hitting him in the head with his rod."

Back by the stern, people were falling all over themselves trying to escape the sea lion.

Another time, Martin was in the back of his boat washing off some small halibut his clients had brought in. He leaned over the back rail.

"This sea lion just shot up from under the boat," said Martin. "He didn't grab anything, but he was right in my face. I fell back right onto my butt, flat on the deck. It was a heart-stopping experience. I guess he saw my hands wiggling and he came to investigate. It happened pretty fast."

In the mid-1980s, Martin said a man named Roy Gould of Anchorage caught the biggest halibut ever with North Country. It weighed 372 pounds.

For years after that, Gould visited Martin at his booth at the annual Great Alaska Sportsman Show and said, "I'm still eating on that halibut."

Mike Coates operates Sorry Charlie Charters with his wife, Laurie. And if "Sorry, Charlie" sounds like a familiar phrase, that's for good reason. Not only did Coates name his business after the boat that had belonged to a deceased friend, but he was well aware of the old humorous cartoon commercials selling tuna fish with the "Sorry, Charlie" punch line.

Coates said he and his wife get along so well running the charter service because, "Our motto is she doesn't clean fish and I don't clean sheets."

Coates always wanted to be a fishing guide, not a diplomat, but sometimes negotiating skills are needed to avoid international incidents that threaten to pop up either on board or back at his lodge when anglers gather for dinner.

Once Coates had some Canadian clients on a week-long trip. Half the group's first language was English, half French. All week Coates heard them sniping at each other periodically. At dinner the night before the last day, things heated up.

"Suddenly, I hear one of them go, 'I know you're talking about us!'" said Coates.

The discussion got louder and he caught words about the Quebec separatist movement. Within minutes, the Coateses were the only ones left at the table.

"The next day," he said, "it was, 'See you later.' No fishing."

Similarly, once Coates had a party consisting of half

Democrats and half Republicans, and he made the mistake of playing Rush Limbaugh's show on the radio. Recipe for conflict.

"All day long it was a political battle," said Coates. "I'm sorry I turned the radio on. Next time I'll play Christmas carols."

Mike Huff of Captain Mike's Charters remembers the time a tiny young woman sang something herself. While fishing for halibut on Huff's boat, she chose to hold her rod between her legs for extra leverage. That was fine until she got a bite. When a big halibut hit, the force raised the pole between her legs.

"The fish lifts her off her feet," said Huff. "She's just dangling there. She let out a hell of a yell. Someone had to pull her down."

Which is not the only time Huff nearly lost an angler overboard.

"A woman was by the railing and she was leaning over, over, over," said Huff. "She had a big fish on and the fish took off. Her feet were above her head. This guy reached out and grabbed her by the jacket and pulled her back. We got the fish, too. It was between a 125-pounder and a 150-pounder. She was probably a 120-pounder."

Sometimes the water gets rough out there on the ocean and on one return trip to Homer, when Huff was coming in from the Barren Islands, the waves were very turbulent.

"We were just launching off the waves," said Huff. "I slowed down coming off a wave and someone was in the bathroom bracing himself. He came down so hard he broke the toilet seat."

Oof.

One of Huff's favorite customers of all time did something that really didn't have much to do with actual fishing. The man sauntered into the crowded charter company's office one day and hushed the mob by asking, "Does my wife need to wear underwear on your boat?"

Mary Huff, Captain Mike's wife, was staffing the office, and she was ready.

"That's entirely up to you," she said. "We don't have a policy on that."

Turns out the man meant long underwear.

Fishing in the Barren Islands on a different trip, Huff said his clients were bringing in halibut of all sizes. His deckhands were throwing the fish into a big storage box at the back of the boat, and after one catch they lifted the lid and got a surprise. One fish, which weighed about 40 pounds, bounced off the deck and back into the water.

All of a sudden, the dead fish began swimming around!

"We're trying to gaff it," said Huff. "It had been in the box at least two hours. Only it swam away. That fish deserved to live. You wouldn't think something like that could ever happen. It was just a nice, healthy fish. Apparently, real healthy. True story."

True story? Famous last words.

KELLY HANKE

About the Author

Lew Freedman is the sports editor of the *Anchorage Daily News*, Alaska's largest daily newspaper, and the author of ten other books about Alaska.

A prize-winning sports writer, Freedman is a native of Boston, Massachusetts, where he attended Boston University. He also has a master's degree from Alaska Pacific University.

Freedman and his wife, Donna, live in Anchorage and are the parents of one daughter, Abigail.